Words of
AFFIRMATION

One man's righteous journey, in his quest for survival

Jacob Josè

INDIA • SINGAPORE • MALAYSIA

ISBN
Paperback: 979-8-88815-302-4
Hardcase: 979-8-89233-525-6

To My Two Fathers

One Eternal & The Other Ethereal

Contents

Foreword

"Adventures do occur, but not punctually," wrote Rudyard Kipling in his 1924 novel Passage to India. Anyone who has travelled a great deal knows that you can plan for almost everything—except adventures. Those happen along the way—and they are usually unexpected. But many of us fail to learn from the very adventures that surprise us on this journey called life. The award-wining author Frederick Buechner (1926–2022) often talked about the importance of "listening to your life". What he meant was that there is much we can learn by reflecting on the things that happen to us. If we just take time to listen, we can become wiser and happier.

Jacob Jose is a man who has learnt a great deal by listening to his life. He honours his father in this work, praising him for his mentorship and the many life-lessons he passed on to him. He also writes about his own adventures during his sojourns in India, Kenya, Singapore, South Africa, Sri Lanka, Thailand and other parts of the world. In this book he takes readers on a journey with him, describing in vivid detail some of the places he has been and a few of the people he has met. Readers will sometimes feel like they are travelling with him—taking in the sights, sounds and scents of distant lands—and having tea in the evening with a friend to talk about the lessons learnt through unexpected adventures. And there is humour in this book. I laughed out loud as I read his story of being so desperate for "divine intervention" that he found himself chasing a priest down a crowded, narrow street somewhere in Sri Lanka as the holy man rode away on his bicycle. It was delightfully entertaining—and a picture of how desperate we all are to unburden our souls to another human being.

I greatly appreciate the beautiful balance Jacob has achieved in this world. He is not cynical—but is certainly not naïve. Few people have been able to find a healthy place between these two extremes. The cunning and corruption of people can leave a person disillusioned—feeling like there is no one they can trust. This worldview is understandable in this broken world, but it is also distorted. There are people you can trust in this life. It is also self-defeating. Without trust we would never go out for a walk, get in a taxi, or buy food at the local market. For that matter, we would never walk out the doors of our house. Prosperous people have learnt that succeeding in this life means that you need people you can count on in business and life. Discernment is the way forward—being able to know who you can and cannot trust. Determination is also important, because you won't always get it right. No one ever does. We have all been betrayed. Everyone has encountered Judas. But you can maintain your character in a cut-throat world. You don't have to become like the people who have wronged you in order to be successful. Jacob tries to point us in this direction.

Jacob also encourages us to look for opportunities to help those around us—even when it seems like we don't have anything to give. He tells a story about being stuck in Sri Lanka due to unexpected delays on a major business project. He had to change travel plans, cancel other commitments, and deal with one unexpected disappointment after another. It was frustrating. But while he was trying to handle headaches and sort out setbacks on the job, an opportunity came his way to volunteer his time and give his resources to help a local parish with a small construction project. In a way, it was the last thing he needed, but he heard his father's affirmations calling him to say yes. To his unexpected delight, not only did he help the local parish build their community centre in the course of giving his time away, but he also forged new friendships with local influencers who were able to help him sort out the problems he was having at work. It was a win-win. "Giving is its own reward", as the expression goes, but Jacob's willingness to give when it wasn't convenient ended up blessing him and his company in ways he could have never foreseen. Jacob believes that life can be a win-win and that we can "take everyone along", to use his expression. He tries to show us a way forward that is good and generous.

This book also offers some helpful warnings. It has been said that "failure has slain its thousands and success has slain its tens of thousands". There are variations of this witty trope which has been loosely borrowed from the Biblical story of King Saul, whose own pride eventually proved to be his undoing. This book warns us about some of the dangers of success—things that can bring a person down. Some of these pitfalls include wealth, women and wine. He is careful to say that there is nothing evil in any of these gifts from the Creator, but there are desires lurking within all of our hearts that tempt us to take what is good and use it in ways that will bring harm. We are right to be careful, to know that we are all vulnerable in some way. Jacob calls us to put wisdom first, before all else, because this will help us stay on the path of prosperity while other voices call out to us.

It will not come as a surprise to anyone who knows Jacob's family story that this is also a book about a man's faith. When I first met Jacob, I was impressed by his willingness to talk openly about what he believed. He did not do this in a way that was arrogant or off-putting. An aura of authentic spirituality is evident in his life, and it is something that informs the way he treats everyone. Because his faith is so central to who he is, it is only expected that he would talk about it. We usually talk about the things that are very important to us! And Jacob does so in a way that is winsome and warm. He is a person with deep personal convictions who also holds charitable views toward everyone he encounters. It is rare in our world today to find people of conviction who are marked by generosity. Jacob strikes a balance that is so desperately needed in contemporary society, and I think this is something readers will hear in his words of affirmation.

The CEO Magazine, one of the most influential media outlets, has described Jacob Jose as someone who is "inspiring the next generation of hardworking professionals". Readers will be inspired by this warm-hearted and uplifting personal memoir. His words of affirmation are also words of inspiration that will help others "listen to their lives" when adventures do occur.

F. Lionel Young III, PhD

Austin, Texas | 2023

***

A word fitly spoken
is like apples of gold
in a setting of silver.
Proverbs 25:11

Acknowledgements

With profound gratitude, I would like to acknowledge the support and love of my family and friends, without which this book would not have seen the light of day.

Lavina, my wife, who believes in my inner strength and continues to inspire me in this journey of life.

God's greatest gift to me, my children Leah and Kian.

To my Grandmother for the Gift of Faith. I miss you every day.

To my Father and Grandfather for their Affirmations.

To my Mother for the Gift of Life.

To every parent, a child's first mentor, may your virtuous words and deeds stand out like a beacon of light that guards against rocky shorelines.

To every child, a parent's first true love, may you see the hidden affirmations in your parents and be an inspiration to everyone in your circle of life!

To you, dear reader, may the affirmations seed in you the zeal to take on this challenging world and uplift those around you.

Preface

This book is based on my understanding of the experiences passed on to me by my father from a mentorship standpoint. Though most of us are blessed with parents who radiate positive affirmations, ironically, not all of us are willing to perceive and embrace those hidden qualities with open arms.

Words of affirmation are words or deeds that transfuse from one person to another and serve as an even keel for affirmations to take self-transcendence in oneself, akin to rising above one's capabilities and exemplifying our very own hidden potential.

Through the affirmations, I delve deeper into self-transcendence, beyond my resentful past, beyond my cowering days faced with corruption, beyond my gruelling formative days with officials deeply laced in fiefdom, beyond my days of sadistic fiends who never valued me for my true worth. Sadly, the landscape remains unscathed even today—beyond my past, shrouded with pain and anguish for the inhumane treatment meted out to a trustworthy, modest individual seeking to make a change in the business environment. Beyond my days globetrotting to make ends meet, sometimes without a proper meal. Beyond my past, when days seemed endless as I had to wait for long—impaling hours to ascertain a firm ground, way beyond my days belabouring the obvious and treacherous.

Like many tireless souls, I too have led an arduous and socially-detached life, one on my own terms. A life of prayers hindered. Though I remained firm about the core principles and values that my grandparents passed on to me, I, just like many of us, young and elderly, struggled to find a guiding light by which I could outdo myself and lead a more meaningful life.

These 'words of affirmation' are some of my father's inherent beliefs and declarations, by which he went on to live a life of fulfilment and achieved the kind of success that only a few could, in continuing to steer an organisation faced with the most significant challenges single-handedly for over three decades and in influencing society at large to lead a life of contentment—especially when down and out. Some of the affirmations he imbibed from my grandfather whom he adulated and revered, while many he penned during his long and arduous journey, inadvertently imbibing me with many of his beliefs.

Discerning the Hidden Affirmations?

With challenges in business unsurmountable, I began to seek divine solace in the hope of finding a solution. Besides, I started to ruminate how successful individuals within the industrial and non-industrial landscapes endured such trials. However, amidst my deep reflection, I realised the futility of my rumination, when it struck me how the Almighty had an answer to some of my life's greatest challenges in my father.

Post my graduation, on a fine morning, discussions about my career with my father over breakfast transpired into one of my most important professional decisions. We were both elated as I had accepted his informal request to be part of his organisation. Culturally, in our part of the world, one would be predominantly scorned in society if a son declined to work in his family-owned business. In contrast, I was firm on not being condoned by my family for overturning an offer, particularly by my father, who had painstakingly built his empire around solid principles and business ethics. His long-cherished desire was for the organisation to continue to thrive and for customers to benefit from our products under my leadership.

The genesis of the company my father founded began around a meal when my parents had decided to part ways from my maternal family's century-old business over a squabble with my maternal grandfather, who was somewhat envious of my parents' fast garnering fame within the manufacturing landscape. My parents then painstakingly pledged everything they had in the hope of raising funds to rent a space and procure machinery to hastily manufacture specific equipment they had assured delivery to their clients before relocating of their own volition. Fast-forward a few years, the company had established itself as a name to reckon with in the specialised steel manufacturing sector.

Well, for my father, not so long into the formative years of his stride in the business landscape, his painstaking efforts bore fruit when he clinched a deal for supplying equipment to one of the country's behemoths in the defence sector. However, his halcyon days of tranquillity, contentment, and prosperity were short-lived since the latter had a decoy plan of convincing my father to design and build an advanced prototype with the assurance of awarding another contract to him for making a hundred more. After taking deliveries of the developed prototype, the officials on the successful commissioning went on to award the rest of the contracts to their favoured vendors by plagiarising my father's designs. It was an early setback that took its toll on my father's mental and physical health while also inciting him to take on the world head-on.

For those who travail, hoping to seek success, none can preclude one's destiny – Jacob Jose.

I secured my future in my father's organisation, starting as a grunt and rapidly climbing my way to the top, ensuring there was no dearth of expertise, no matter the challenges. During my seminal years, it was natural for me to work in the engineering division as I had a flair for complex design and problem-solving in related domains. Besides, there was no better way I could get to the nadir of understanding our core product and its relationship with other functioning divisions, especially manufacturing, which served as the backbone for our timely and stellar performance in the various industries we catered to.

Overwhelmed by the colossal scale of structures we were fabricating, I was left awestruck by my father's dedication in building the institution with over two hundred employees, that too on an even keel—the very foundation that would help me continue his unwavering legacy. These structures and equipment would then be erected at various locations, requiring us to travel to every nook and corner of the world, thus enabling us to build experience on how businesses operated around the globe.

Not too long into my foray into business operations, I realised maintaining deadlines and the excellent reputation we enjoyed as a premium vendor demanded the character and skillset well beyond our technical superiority and quality workmanship. The accolades we received from our clients on the completion of projects on one side were balanced by the shrewd business actions of our competitors on the other. I copiously comprehended, by observing my father at work from close quarters, that to run a successful and purposeful business, one certainly had to possess innate traits or emulate beliefs and qualities passed on to them from a person they held in good stead. Besides, one had to keep abreast of developments in the industry and constantly innovate by acquiring new strategies to generate profits and enrich employees' lives and the environment we live in. In a way, I could ascribe my father's perseverance, resilience, and success to his affirmations.

As luck would have it, my perspective on life broadened when I embarked on this incredible journey called the African sojourn.

Before I move on to my two-decade-long transformative journey, I want to address a question that sparks fear in the minds of industrialists and businessmen: 'What would you do if a bigwig decided to compete in your sector?'

These days, smaller business firms can be easily replaced or acquired by any of the behemoths around—Keiretsus or Zaibatsus of Japan, Chaebols of South Korea, Qiyejituans of China, American MNCs, British business empires, the German Mittelstands, or even the Indian business houses. Some 40 summers ago, when my father first saw the signs of the bulk material handling industry showing promise, he charted a new path. His key focus on product simplicity, safety, and efficiency enabled him and his unwavering team to drive the business successfully on a global scale. However, corruption and business rivalry remained his most significant challenges to surmount.

Nevertheless, with the passage of time, I realised how one man's affirmations laid a strong foundation and shaped not just my future but the future of many who were graced by it. In a way, my father's affirmations are the subtle cues to question: 'What would you do if a bigwig decides to compete with or acquire you?' or 'How would you sail through a precarious situation faced with corruption or competition?'

Moving on to corruption, has anyone or any industry or business not had to deal with corruption? Be it bribery, lobbying, cronyism, nepotism, parochialism, or influence peddling. We have all been hit by it at some point in time or the other. Corruption goes by different names across the globe. If you do not play along, the 'game' gets more intense and focused on destroying you.

Like corruption, we too are lured into unethical business scenarios where tough choices need to be considered, none of which seems to invariably resolve the problem within accepted ethical guidelines.

Most of us have encountered such situations in almost every aspect of our lives, including personal, social, and professional. To reiterate, it could involve an employee, a colleague, members of a cohort, a business acquaintance, a government official, or even a family member.

The biggest challenge related to corruption or ethical dilemmas is not about offering a solution that complies with the perpetrator's demands or needs – but traversing away from the paths of these immoral guilds by scorning their very fundamentals. People have faced such dilemmas throughout history, and philosophers have striven to find solutions to resolve them – but with limited success.

Let's cut to the chase. In both contexts, i.e., competing with an industry heavyweight or facing a moral issue, I must admit that my father's hidden affirmations, attributable to his devout upbringing, have redeemed not just me and my loved ones but many others from undesirable situations.

At some point in your life, you may have come across people of a rare kind, a kind that you might never see again, men and women who live their lives perfectly, attain success in everything they do and overcome a myriad of challenges with ease—and you may have wondered how they do it. In contrast, many of us languish in dismay and remain stranded throughout our personal or professional lives. *Words of Affirmation* is a delicately crafted read on how to overcome some of our greatest challenges and lead a life of not just success but contentment. The affirmations, when imbibed, can help break stereotypes and achieve greatness beyond one's imagination.

To give you a heads-up, here are the key takeaways from this book:

- How can sexual austerity be integrated into your professional and personal life for greater success?
- Given a choice, what would you prefer first and what would be your order of preference - Wine, Women, Wealth, or Wisdom?
- Another intriguing subject is how one can deal with truth and lust.

  and much more...

These affirmations are a roadmap to seeding in oneself the enthusiasm to look out for hidden affirmations in people from all walks of life. This book is for all who wish to discover their very own affirmations. In a way, it also aims to empower every reader to look out for hidden affirmations within.

Penning about my journey, chronicling the profound impact my father had on my life and how his adept use of affirmations served as a steadfast source of strength during the most challenging phase of my life. His relentless pursuit of surmounting the challenges that lay ahead, harnessing the power of affirmations by cultivating positivity, and achieving success inspired many in society.

Over time, he generously imparted these values to me and many who idolised him. With his guidance and unwavering commitment, the affirmations served as an impetus towards my entrepreneurial success.

During the intricate tapestry of my life, the assertions remained a constant source of enlightenment and resilience.

I started my own long and insightful journey during my African sojourn, a journey on which the ten of my father's most significant affirmations began taking effect during my formative years, making me not just a successful entrepreneur but a better father, husband and mentor!

I hope *Words of Affirmation* will be an interesting read and help you reap the benefits it extols until we meet again on my next journey.

***

From Father to Son

Wisdom is knowing the right path to take.
Integrity is taking it.

M.H. McKee

During the late 1920s, determined to fend off colonial atrocity in his tiny hamlet, a young minor was held captive and subjected to trial by ordeal for being part of a protest that was unworthy of its citing.

Against the backdrop of public outcry and massacres, the youngster and his circle of friends waded past a large crowd of political demonstrators to witness the drama unfolding at the behest of the ruling colonists. The profoundly motivated youngsters, for once, never thought their actions would place them in the vanguard of a powerful transformation that would go on to sweep their lands.

Wrestling among the crowds and on reaching the forefront of the demonstrations, the youngster and his circle questioned one of the guards as to why they pushed a young woman since it was taboo during the colonial era for men to touch women, let alone manhandle them. The guard in question nodded while looking at his fellow guards. 'These kids?' before throwing a blow at the youngster. It was the start of a violent protest that ensued, enraging the demonstrators of the small town.

It all began when peaceful activists had gathered to condemn the burning of khadi clothes by the imperial police officers at the command of their high-ranking officials. The protestors were further manhandled and ill-treated by the abhorrent police officers while creating an awareness of the cultural and economic significance of khadi clothes since many household members would hand weave them, inevitably reducing the country's dependency on foreign textiles. Besides, hand weaving provided an alternate income for many during the hot and arid summers as the populace was predominantly agrarian.

On the one hand, the colonists exported heavily bargained and locally produced raw materials and re-imported machine-finished textiles, inundating the once-flourishing local textile industry and selling them at much higher prices. On the other hand, they would endorse their goods by discouraging the prevailing local cottage industry by intimidation to ensure their imported textiles sold locally reaped higher profits. On the contrary, though affordable, the locally produced goods whose hallowed designs and embroidery were renowned for millennia, which once proliferated the European textile market, were heavily taxed and deprived of being exported overseas, thus driving the country's once-flourishing trade to the brink of economic upheaval. Such were the colonists' obscene mercantile policies that rendered the local community jobless, irking many nationwide.

The minor protestor decided to take the discriminatory and bigoted actions of the Imperial police head-on. The violence and gore that ensued left the young teenager blinded in one eye. Perhaps the idea of desisting colonial laws led to aggression by the latter, replete with torrents of vile abuse and persecution.

News of the young, wounded teenager had spread far and wide, with arrests looming at large; the local head and village representative, whose nephew was the factually innocent and ostensible convict, desperately tried to salvage his reputation and coveted position with the colonists, covertly translocated the youngster to a neighbouring state to be treated at a private Christian community. The youngster was dropped off at a train station with essential treatment to survive the overnight journey before taking refuge at an infirmary run by an American missionary.

Though hitherto well poised and composed to have his vision back, despite the doctors' ostensible persuasion to calm the young patient before surgery with the conviction there was nothing they could do to salvage the vile abuse borne by the eye, the youngster began showing signs of anxiety sensing something awry, much to their very obtuse. The youngster was witty and astute in every sense; he was aware of losing his vision in one eye.

For the next six months, while at the centre, the young solitary convalescent imbibed life-altering lessons from an American missionary who founded the Christian community, which saved his life, but sadly not his eye. The institutor, Ms. Ida Scudder, was from a family of missionaries who globetrotted and witnessing sufferance due to the lack of treatment centres, especially for women, led to the genesis of this present-day renowned medical centre. She went on to dedicate her life to the service of the country and mankind. The young convalescent learnt some of his virtues from her while many others by himself, especially while contemplating his past actions while in solitary convalesce.

Of the many lessons he learnt, the one he spoke to me with profound emotion was when I asked him – "Did you ever forgive the colonists?" His reply was certainly without a tad of resentment towards them, and his deep grin illuminated everyone around him. His response almost bore the resemblance of '*learn to forgive*'.

Over the years, the young protestor was a paragon of virtue, and some of the ideals that shaped him were his affirmations that would influence the lives of many he touched.

How did I meet the young teenager? Or how did he influence my life? Fast-forward six decades – he was my paternal grandfather, whose exemplary way of life helped us elevate our comprehension of solving some of life's most significant challenges, underscoring the magnitude of his affirmations.

Some of my grandfather's and father's affirmations continue to guide me in stewarding the key decisions of my life responsibly. Words do matter, but more importantly, the choice of words matters most! Those words of affirmation stand out like a beacon of light that guards against rocky shorelines.

To some, words may seem meaningless, but to others, beneath each word is an ocean of meaning and significance that manoeuvres every step in the journey of life. For people like me, who gravitate towards words of affirmation, I find them comforting, and this feeling has been strengthened because of the positive reinforcement that these words have provided to many people I have come across, lighting their paths.

In the life of any accomplished businessperson, their character stands out, not when they are faring reasonably well, but when they are down and out. My father, while encountering his most significant challenges, disposed of a persona of someone highly determined and unflustered, especially while facing the wrath of rivals & renegades—a rarity in today's fast-paced times. When any argument or position with opponents alike was untenable, it required someone astute and hard-headed to carry out the most obscure modus operandi; my father was an embodiment of solving such complex challenges. When the system that purports to protect or support us turned hostile, my father ensured these cruel edicts sunk into obscurity. When the world was facing an enduring financial calamity by the onset of the great recession, my father never once fulminated; he was fiery on the marketing and sales front, but back home or at his workplace, his disposition was with the Zen of a Buddhist monk. He held his family and workers with such high stead.

When someone antagonised him with utter contempt, he barely reacted as though it was well below his worth. When his adult life was blighted with frequent physical illness and suffering, he exuded an aura of dexterity and patience. My father's life in many a way underscores the significance of solving some of our life's ever-burgeoning problems. He was an endearing personality.

While I meditate upon how a man could endure so much suffering while exuding such calm, I began to realise that he was, in a way, blessed with splendid mental agility and an exuberant vitality, perhaps tolerant to challenges, almost of extravagance. Though I began to realise my father's 'Life's Passage' a bit late, I'm glad I was never too late!

It all began in the early summer of 2004 when I started taking a keen interest in my father's structural design, fabrication, and bulk material handling business. Unfortunately, in my enthusiasm to earn my place rather too quickly, I began to rush into many ill-informed decisions. As I understood my follies, I set out to understand my father's successful approach and realised that it was his underlying hidden affirmations that could be credited with his unerring decision-making skills. These affirmations went on to help guide me away from toxic relationships, business pitfalls, unethical practices, habitual weaknesses, trivial shortcomings, and the like.

Just like everyone else, my father's business began with a dream. Some dreams are big and ambitious. Others are modest and realistic. My father's aspirations fell somewhere in between when he established his business venture some 40 summers ago, in the early 1980s.

On the one hand, my father wanted to build a sustainable business with a steady and predictable revenue stream. But, on the other hand, he truly wanted to create a business that was impactful at scale, one that would provide equipment and turnkey solutions to industries relying mainly upon bulk material handling equipment. The company's products were designed and built to allow easy maintenance to promote simplicity, safety, and efficiency. A constant quest for excellence has made the company one of the best in the field of bulk material handling. A rarity in the business landscape then, and sadly, all the more so today.

Coming back to my father's business, fast-forward 40 years, we've catered to hundreds of clients who have given us millions of pounds in revenue and product installations spanning 40 countries and growing. It is pertinent to mention that mission-critical values embedded within the organisation have helped build sustainable relationships with employees or customers.

Tempting as it is for me to think that we've made it, it was my father's sage advice to stay grounded—for the long haul—that served as the beginning of the tutelage I received from a good father and a great alchemist! I was in awe of his realm of thought, be it of the materialistic world or, on the contrary, the spiritual world. His words and actions were more ethereal and resonated with his affirmations.

To take you through the journey, here are ten of my father's key affirmations, which guided me as a beacon of light against adversaries and adversities. It all began with the African sojourn.

The African Sojourn

Knowledge without wisdom is like water in the sand.

African proverb

As humans, we have a fundamental urge to find a relationship with the cosmos, not just in metaphysical but also in spiritual terms. During the summer of 2015, I began to foray into my spiritual journey. I would pray fervently, mainly for a breakthrough in business, following the footsteps of my father, who would always seek divine intervention, especially during trying times. The days ahead appeared uncertain, with changing market dynamics; it was challenging, with our survival at stake.

Most of the time, the answers to our prayers are hidden in plain sight. We see the signs, and we connect the dots.

Et voilà!

At times, the calling is more often veiled, and, as believers, we are duty-bound to look for these ethereal signs.

Without further ado, here is a short recap of every major event that transpired during the transition phase of my career.

It all began on my 33rd birthday with an early morning visit to my parish, a short, pleasant drive from home. It was inveterate for me to attend early morning prayers as the routine had a litany of hidden treasures – the cool morning breeze, the quiet and desolate streets, the tolling of church bells, the evocative scents of the incense, the smoke of smouldering balsamic resins, the numerous luminous flames of the votive candles, finally culminating with the exchange of greetings with the religious and elderly church regulars, all of which had a calming effect on my otherwise turbulent mind commensurate with my hectic work schedule.

Feeling invigorated, I returned home for a quick breakfast and pampering from my loved ones. I headed straight to work and ensured I was on time, as it was traditional for me to be greeted upon arrival by all my colleagues.

Surprisingly, the cheer and applause that ensued on my arrival, with employees raining me with rose petals, was a fervid moment. The cheerful hysteria by my colleagues was the manifestation of many years of dedication by my father to the institution he built. It was their manner of reciprocating for all my father's contributions, sacrifices, and selfless service.

After the formal greeting by 400-odd co-workers, my feet teetered as I was excited beyond measure by their roaring welcome and allegiance. As the euphoria abated – without halting for a moment, I proceeded straight to my office cabin to settle down with the events recurring in my mind, entranced by the humbling gesture I had just received. As I sat on my reclining chair, lulled by the sounds of trickling water from the nearby fountain, my eyes intuitively fixated on the glass tabletop – beneath the transparent impervious layer was a printout of the vision statement of my father's organisation. I pondered upon the depth of his passion for the products he designed and the customers he served while always ensuring to enrich the lives of his employees. I was still in a daze about living up to his expectations and carrying forward his unwavering legacy.

While immersed in these thoughts, my telephone rang abruptly, drawing my attention. It was a call from my father, asking me to come over to his plush office cabin for a board meeting to be presided over by him.

Nostalgic as it may sound, I was also expecting it to be a greeting from my father, which was usually a customary annual affair – a peck on my cheek and a warm lingering hug – that I would be eagerly awaiting each year! Entering his opulent yet welcoming cabin, I saw his vivid smile and the radiant glow on his face, which I attribute to his inner spiritual strength in the face of all his personal and professional challenges. His unfailing courtesy and warmth during any situation always left me and many others perplexed. How could someone ever be so peaceful in today's fast-paced world? Seated opposite him was our company's COO and my father's most trusted companion over the last decade, who incidentally was also my mentor and guide. I fondly call him VKG. My family's other two board members could not make it that day.

After my father's customary annual greetings, I sat opposite him and beside my COO. The ensuing commotion within the HR and finance teams as they prepared some papers for the scheduled meeting startled me and ignited a sense of anxiety about what would happen next. On the contrary, I could, in a way, sense a surprise around the corner. Nevertheless, I kept myself calm, not showing any signs of distress or excitement. I held onto my thoughts and let the events play out on their own.

It was the 19th day of November. The winter dew was settling on the large panoramic window pane behind my father's desk, overlooking the prized mango trees he had planted almost three decades ago, embellishing the view from his third-floor office. With the chirping of birds and hopping of squirrels on the branches, I realised how sacred this space must have been to him and his affinity for the trees he had planted, which had grown from tiny saplings to towering trees (that stand tall even today). Reminiscing the summers I spent as a child, I couldn't help being wistful about my time watering these tiny saplings to measuring their growth against mine. The place resonated with the spirit of my father's lifelong struggles and passion.

Before I could speak up, a colleague brought in a set of papers my father handed over, asking me to sign them. When I inquired what they were, he replied that he was formally handing over the reins to me! He and my COO mentioned that I was best suited for the role, considering my decade-and-a-half years of experience, despite the mistakes I've made, which were the stepping stones to my steep learning that would keep me resilient in this industry. It felt like a double whammy to me: a moment of ambivalence; on the one hand, the industry was in a muddle and, on the other, my father was handing over his most prized possession – especially when I felt I could do with a little more mentoring before taking over the realms of this great institution. Spiritually speaking, it was a 'baptism by fire.' Surprised though as I was by this, there was another shocking revelation in store for me – of how their decision to give a minor stake to a major reputed organisation never materialised – as the latter had never found our offer lucrative.

Though I was aware of the developments, I was not privy to the extent of the discussions. The times were tough and highly challenging for the industry, and we, too, were no exception. With liquidity almost running dry, we could barely make ends meet. In simple words, we were in the throes of an economic recession that was too deep for self-revival.

An hour later, a formal takeover announcement was made to the employees gathered at a joint meeting area, culminating in a two-fold surprise celebration. As the day ended, a group of around 20-odd workers requested my secretary for a personal meeting. They were waiting at the exit gate to greet me.

These were the very men who began their careers with my father. They had served the organisation for over 30 long years. It is pertinent to mention that each of them had carried me when I was an infant. I had noticed how these iron workers had worked hard and persevered all these years, their wrinkled and tanned skin testament to their sheer grit and efforts. Before I could leave, they wished me the best and shared their sense of pride over the fact that all their work had not gone in vain. They were also glad they could continue serving the organisation under my leadership.

Humbled by their gesture, I thanked them and walked towards my car. Emotions were running high, and I could see tears of joy in the eyes of my chauffeur. Even before I could enquire about them, he quickly closed the door, which was probably a sign that he was shy about his emotions.

My next stop… home.

I was still in a daze, contemplating whether I could play the cards like my father had dealt and how I could innovate to help our company and its stakeholders navigate the financial turmoil.

Looking for solutions to the various problems at hand, I began by treading the spiritual path.

It all changed one fine morning while I was partaking in a prayer session at a spiritual centre not far from home. The hallowed space was at peak capacity, filled with people from all walks of life. It did not take long for my hawked eye to recognise their disposition and demeanour as I, too, was sailing through the same troubled waters. The space had an aura of deliverance, while the worshippers had a gravitas of belief, which was clearly apparent for all to witness. Many proclaimed their blessings, while many hoped for a miracle in desperation. It is true that sometimes, in life, hope is all that you can hold on to. I saw many battered souls asking for his mercy, a sliver of light in the darkest dungeons.

While in deep prayer and pure contrition, I suddenly felt my chair shudder and heard a feeble ringtone. It took a while for me to realise that it was my phone. I ignored it initially, but after a couple of minutes, I reluctantly took a cursory look at the phone and noticed that I had missed a few calls – due to the high-pitched chants around me. I realised it was an international number, and someone from overseas was frantically trying to reach out to me. Although it was tempting to return the call, I had to ignore it since answering the phone during a worship session is considered disrespectful. I went back to reciting the prayers and completely forgot about it as I was lost in the euphoria.

Later that evening, as I stepped out of the spiritual centre, I intuitively returned the call. The phone kept ringing at the other end. Just as I was about to disconnect, I heard a low-pitched voice say, 'Hello.'

It was from an old business acquaintance of ours from East Africa, enquiring about our company's interest in the prospect of executing a project in East Africa.

It struck me then.. how an opportunity can emerge from nowhere! This got me thinking about what my father intensely voiced to me about the affirmations. I realised that God had heard my prayers and comprehended my father's words of wisdom: 'If you believe in prayers, God will certainly hear your call!'

Over a meal the following evening, I discussed this opportunity with my father, my idea being to send my sales head out there, but then he suggested that I explore the business potential myself. I was, however, not too keen to go there by myself, as the country was going through a tumultuous period of terrorism and civil strife. Personally, I was in deep anguish, as this period also coincided with my fourth attempt at fatherhood, with three of the previous efforts not having gone on expected lines. I was considering the odds and in no frame of mind to travel to that part of the world yet.

Today, the more I think about it, the more I feel it was a calling!

Notwithstanding my reservations, I heeded the providential call and embarked on my journey to East Africa. It was the beginning of an experience that led to my gaining truly insightful knowledge and wisdom through his words of affirmation.

Africa!

As the name springs to our minds with images of vast jungles and savannahs, highlands and deserts, rivers, and creeks, known to all explorers as the dark continent, my maiden African sojourn had a distinct yet enchanting side to my mnemonic imagination.

Oppressed by colonisation and loot that catalysed the once peaceful savannah with a chain of events rendering the populace lacking bare necessities, disease, poverty, riots, rape, and pillage, post the years of thraldom the world portrays it with, the Africa that met my eyes transcended every notion that echoes through their mystic lands. While the world ascribes Africa to ghoulish atrocities, bouts of repeated violence, appallingly inhumane living conditions, and many more vile attributes - through my sojourn, the intricate caricature of living in a developed world's ostensible luxuries became furthermore evident by the latter's cultural and moral fractures woven through the contours of their relatively poignant lives filled with loneliness, alienation, and worldly obsession.

The phenomena that struck me the most - during the journey - were the people I met, the encounters I had, and the moments I experienced - all of which were a total reassertion of his words of affirmation! Each of the affirmations came alive in the form of real-life incidents as the events played out by themselves.

***

The Power of Observation

Show respect even to people who don't deserve it; not as a reflection of their character, but as a reflection of yours.

Dave Willis

It all began on a chilly morning. Dashing for my car to escape the pouring rain and the wintry gales, my African sojourn started on a cold note. Traversing the South Asian bustling cityscape with inert beings, devoid of verdure, reminiscent of the many lost souls treading through life with no clear direction and purpose. Overwhelmed by the incessant honking of cars, bumper-to-bumper traffic, and frustrated daily commuters, it appeared as though humanity had lost its way—teeming with hate and contempt. Looking through a raindrop that appeared as a cyclops, magnifying the surroundings, it struck me, as though nature was crying out about the raw deal it was being handed over under the pretext of the city's growth and development.

On reaching the swanky new airport, gazing at the shimmering glass edifice with its striking features had an entrancing effect on me, and at the heart of this magnificent piece of architecture were chandeliers with lights pulsing and flickering, providing an enchanting feel to the passengers besides brightening their spirits as Christmas vacations were around the corner.

I dashed to the immigration counter as I planned to spend some time fine-tuning my company presentation at the lounge prior to boarding my flight. As I rode the escalator towards the upper immigration floor, I noticed an unusual swarm of passengers queuing in front of the 20-odd immigration counters. I wondered whether a few would end up missing their flights due to the unexpectedly long queues. I quickly looked for the fastest-moving queue and headed straight for it.

When I had reached the halfway mark of the long queue, an officer seated at the counter walked up to me and asked to form a new queue at the priority counter reserved for cabin crew—to ease the rush of new passengers arriving on the immigration floor. I headed there without a pause, delighted to be right in front of the newly formed queue.

While I proceeded to have my passport stamped, the officer at the counter requested me to step aside. Before I could gather my wits about what was happening, I noticed he was giving the right of way to the cabin crew, who had just arrived at their priority gate for the immigration check.

As I strode out of the queue, one of the over-courteous air hostesses requested if they could pass by, to which I gently obliged. Little did I realise that one of my father's most significant affirmations took form at that very moment.

An hour later, there was a boarding announcement for our flight. It was an economy class ticket that I had requested my secretary to book, considering my organisation's dire financial situation. Besides, I wanted to set an example by following a series of stringent austerity measures that I had implemented after my takeover. Naïve as it may sound, the string of restraints proved beneficial in the long run.

I walked through the aerobridge to the aircraft's entrance and was greeted by the flight steward, who saw my boarding card and ushered me to take the last right and proceed down the aisle. The flight was unoccupied, as I was among the first to board. I headed straight to my row, following the signs, and placed my hand baggage in the overhead compartment. Just as I was about to shut the compartment, I saw a familiar face next to me and realised it was the same air hostess I had bumped into at the immigration counter earlier. Greeting me, she politely asked if she could place my blazer in the closet, and I gladly offered it with a sigh of relief, as I would not have to worry about its safekeeping in the cramped overhead box.

Just then, a strong whiff of body odour wafted up from my co-passenger, inciting in me an osmophobic reaction.

A few minutes later, most passengers had boarded the aircraft, and the usual commotion of settling down was underway. I was uncomfortable in the two-seater row with my co-passenger, and to make matters worse, I was at the rear end of the aircraft, with his body odour giving me a migraine. I reminisced about my childhood days, during which I had the entire four-seater rows to myself during overseas vacations with the family. Back to the present: the odour was unbelievably overbearing, and I was contemplating a change of seat.

Now, almost everyone had settled down in the aircraft, and my discomfort was growing. The air hostess probably sensed it and realised something was amiss. She quickly walked up to me and enquired if I needed something, and I instantly replied, 'A change of seat.' Curtly greeting my co-passenger, I quickly headed to the four-seater row that she ushered me to. I had all four seats to myself! Unfortunately, before I could savour my new spacious bedstead, I was deprived of this momentary bliss, as one of the passengers greeted me with a big smile and occupied the other aisle seat of my four-seater row. She was a well-groomed young lady of African descent.

A few minutes into the flight, just after the seat belt signs had been turned off, the cabin crew began preparations for the onboard service. I decided to head to the restroom quickly before they occupied the aisles with their food trolleys. Incidentally, I ran into the same air hostess, and I perceived curiosity in her question about why I had requested a change of seat. Before I could reply, she shared an interesting titbit with me; she told me that body odour played a vital role in certain African cultures. She further revealed how some tribes were proud of their scents! It was a matter of pride for some. Culturally, the sense of smell was vital, and the scent was considered an essence of personal identity, allowing members of one tribe to differentiate themselves from others on the continent.

I was quite astonished by her sharp sense of observation.

She went on to elucidate how studies had revealed that animals could smell danger from afar. For example, a mouse could smell a cat, and a vervet monkey could smell an approaching leopard. Likewise, in Africa, elephants could tell members of one tribe herd from another by smell.

The Masai tribe in Africa has been known for centuries as a tribe of fearsome hunters and warriors. By the mid-19th century, the Masai territory was at its largest, extending over modern-day Kenya and half of Tanzania, and body odour among tribe members was a prized symbol.

In Kenya's Amboseli region, the Masai warriors show off their virility by spearing elephants, while the Kamba tribe, who are predominantly agriculturists, leave the giant creatures alone. There are instances when the scent of a garment worn by a Masai tribesman warded off a herd of elephants as compared to the scent of garments worn by a Kamba tribesman.

Returning to my seat, my path crossed with the African gentleman I had snubbed earlier. I got into a conversation with him, and during our exciting discussion, I realised how down-to-earth he was. I instantly regretted the seat change and reflected on the fact that I could have had a wonderful conversation over the next five hours on the flight had I continued sitting beside him. Nevertheless, after learning that he was an Olympian marathoner, I expressed admiration for his achievements on the international stage. As athletes always sweat it out on the field, I observed his sporting nature, yet his face showed no struggle of hurdles. On the contrary, his chiselled and muscular frame spoke volumes about his focused attitude at the highest level in his chosen field. I was in awe of his tenacity and endurance, which came out starkly during our brief exchange.

I was repentant because I had misjudged a person by his odour without observing that he was a thoroughbred gentleman. How much I could have learnt about the world of sports and his culture had I not been impulsive in my decision to ask for a change of seat!

During the long and arduous flight, my mind returned to my father's wise words: *'Don't be impulsive, since words once spoken can never be retrieved and actions undone.'*

In a short while, a flight attendant approached our aisle to serve us our meals. To my dismay, the meal that I preferred was unavailable. Already exhausted from my earlier flight to Dubai, I was famished, since I hadn't had much time between my flights. After serving me a vegetarian meal, the air hostess dashed back to bring me a fruit croissant from business class as an apology for not serving my meal of choice. The fruit croissant was the best I had relished in any of my flights. Kudos to Emirates for the lip-smacking treat.

I had developed the habit of arranging the items on the used platter neatly after finishing my meal, with the silver foil covering the food tray. Likewise, the napkins and face towelettes were neatly folded. Anyone could have mistaken it at first glance for an unused food tray. I noticed my co-passenger looking at me intently, her eyes tearing up and a big smile on her face. When the air hostess approached my row to collect the food tray, she was surprised to see how well it had been arranged. She thanked me, saying she had seen only a handful of passengers rearranging the used food tray the way I had done. As I saw it, it was a mark of respect, not just for the person serving my meal but also for the food that I had savoured, another trait instilled in me by my father.

A couple of hours into the flight, we were ready for touchdown; my not-so-distant lady co-passenger and I had struck up a conversation by then. I didn't want to repeat the mistake I had made with my previous co-passenger. After we disembarked from the aircraft into the East African nation, things were a bit chaotic and unorganised at every stage of the exit process—from immigration to baggage claim. My co-passenger made it a point to stay beside me. Before we left the airport, the co-passenger asked me if I required a SIM card, as I was new to the country. She helped me choose a good network package, making sure I didn't get conned by various hoarders trying to sell unreliable packages. She also asked if I needed a taxi and moved to the far end of the arrival counter, choosing probably the best taxi service provider. Impressed, I asked why she hadn't chosen the previous three taxi counters, to which she replied saying that they were a bunch of conmen who overcharged passengers.

While I was moved again by her over-courteousness, out of curiosity, I enquired about her profession, and she replied that she was an air hostess with the same airline we had just flown and was heading home for a vacation. She went on to add that it was hard for her to believe how carefully I had rearranged the food tray. She said, 'Never in my career has someone shown a flight attendant respect the way you did.' I quickly realised her courteousness did not have to do with being a good-natured person or a steward but was an expression of her gratitude.

The keen powers of observation demonstrated by the air hostesses served as an important lesson for me.

One had observed my reaction to the body odour of my co-passenger, and both had observed my amiable acceptance of a meal I had not chosen and the way I had rearranged my food tray after using it. I realised that their keen sense of observation came from years of practice and experience, not just in their professional but also in their personal lives. In other words, the African lady's respect towards her co-passenger was not only a feature of the skill set associated with her profession but also a reflection of her inherent character.

I reflected on how some of my father's judgements turned out to be prophetic. His keen sense of observation was either a gift or an acquired skill from life's experiences. I am sure that, if my father had been in my place on that flight, his gesture towards my athletic co-passenger would have been different from mine.

Observing my father from close quarters, I've come to realise that self-awareness is a quintessential trait of any born leader. An upright leader must be a good observer. And being a good observer is about more than just self-awareness. While observing oneself is essential, noticing others provides deeper insights to absorb, assimilate, and act on accordingly. Observing others along with oneself creates richer insights to use, which anyone can adopt to survive against the odds, especially during trying circumstances.

I bade adieu to the young African lady before moving on with my journey of discovery and exploration.

***

The Indian Jealousy

Jealousy is the tribute mediocrity pays to genius.

Fulton J. Sheen

While jealousy is not exclusive to any particular culture or community, my father always spoke to me about the intensity with which it is channelled, particularly in a business setting. Around the world, this equation is skewed towards businessmen or professionals who haven't really worked on the tenets of business etiquette.

Upon my arrival in Nairobi, the capital city of Kenya, the taxi dropped me off at the Radisson Upper Hill, a plush hotel in a bustling commercial hub overshadowed by skyscrapers. After a quick meeting with a local representative of a leading firm that helped me gain some valuable insights about the conglomerate I was to meet with during the week, I retired to a secluded corner of the hotel's outdoor patio. From there, I could hear faint sounds, not realising that they were hymns from the nearby church. Sprightly and inquisitive, I set off in the direction of the music, which had a soothing effect on my otherwise wearing mind due to my constant pondering as to where I was headed, that too, in this faraway land.

On getting to the church, I was greeted by a young girl selling fresh fruits from the local farm. She was extremely polite, ever so respectful with a calm demeanour. Surprisingly, her beaded hair appeared as though they were the rhumb lines helping me navigate through the uncharted waters. Without a doubt, my instincts proved to be right. The first sentence that she quipped was, '*Welcome to Africa, the land of opportunities*', while offering me a basket full of fresh produce. Well, she probably knew that I was a foreigner, but for me, I had an answer to the question that had plagued my mind all through the journey to the great African land.

On reaching the vestibule, I sneaked a glance through the window into this calm edifice; the sunset had spilt its rays into the hallway of the Don Bosco church, which caught my attention. I entered this beautiful yet serene sanctuary and was sublimed by the tranquil oasis of holiness and purity, further entrenching my belief in the African sojourn. After spending some time in solitude and asking Almighty for his direction, I returned to the Radisson Upper Hill for supper before calling it a night.

Early the next morning, I headed back to the airport to catch my flight to my next destination, a county far west of the capital city of Nairobi. Upon touchdown, we were greeted by pleasant showers thanks to Lake Victoria. I had read of it as one of Africa's largest freshwater lakes and the source of the White Nile. Exiting the small yet beckoning airport, I met my chauffeur named Sammy, who was elated to meet his new passenger. It was a three-and-a-half-hour drive to my hotel, and without wasting a moment, we were deep in conversation.

It was only during my drive through the county that I realised the sheer size of this great lake that is shared by three countries. I was overwhelmed when Sammy mentioned that I was witnessing just the tip of the iceberg. He went on to add that the lake was spread across an area the size of Ireland.

During the three-hour drive to the picturesque county, he slowed down at a spot and walked me to the edge of the lake that was placid while the sun glinted off the top of the small ripples. It was here that I witnessed one of the most breathtaking sights Mother Nature had to offer. The flamboyance of hundreds of thousands of flamingos feeding their offspring, spreading their wings, and pecking each other. As I headed close to a flock of ducks, who upon sensing danger took flight in a trice, forcing me to duck down. I was further startled by the sight of geese flying overhead in a 'V' formation, appearing as though victory was imminent. I was humbled beyond words while drawing admiration from these weary beings who endured harsh weathers migrating from afar to find an unrestrained spot amongst nature to breed and thrive, before returning with their offspring.

A couple of hours later, we were at the hotel; I bid my chauffeur goodbye. I was touched by the wise words he whispered: '*This land has been the same since God's creation.' He had felt my awe.*

As it was a bit late in the afternoon, I decided to get my 40 winks in a nice bed carved out of African mahogany, only to be awoken by the sound of the national bird—the lilac-breasted roller. It was such a pleasant treat to hear the bird hum. I had heard nothing like it before.

Later that evening, I walked along the fringes of the forest and found it very pleasing, especially because the showers had ceased. The day continued with a visit to the local market in the nearby town.

The sights of the religious processions, tiny tots swinging to tribal music, and teens kicking around a gunny-sack football that were common across the town were humbling and evoked timeless memories of my childhood. People were grooving to music early in the day at every nook and corner. I had never witnessed anything of this sort. It was indeed a culture shock, and the visit sparked a great sense of gratitude in me.

What inspired me the most was that people in this remote town, desolate and bereft of any resources or luxuries, lived their lives with such contentment and joy. I was reminded of what my father fondly spoke of his childhood days, a time he always reminisced about. The contrast with today's generation, in which people seek opulence and instant gratification, is sad.

I stopped to try out some local cuisine before heading back to my hotel for a late sunset coffee. Without wasting much time, I dashed to the hotel lawn for a moment of solitude while faint music from the town lingered in the background. There was so much positive energy and benevolence that I noticed among the people in this remote and picturesque valley.

While I was transfixed by the sunset, the touch of a warm hand on my shoulder quickly awakened me. Standing behind my recliner was a stranger of Indian origin who probably knew about my intention to visit the conglomerate. He was a towering personality, not just in physique but also at heart, which I only realised over the years.

After our brief introduction, I requested him to join me for a cup of coffee, while both of us enjoyed the African sunset overlooking the pristine hills. It had been almost four decades since his first visit here, and he mentioned how nothing much had changed in this magnificent valley, where time stood still. He recounted how he, along with the chairman of the conglomerate and a colonel during the late 1980s, had looked at the same valley from the chairman's bungalow over a cup of coffee!

Incidentally, I can sense a strong aroma of African coffee beans as I write this book!

The gentleman briefed me on how he was chosen to work with the founder of one of East Africa's leading business conglomerates. He further explained how he had to give up everything in his country of origin and relocate to help the founder set up an industry and manage his day-to-day personal affairs. I wondered what must have gone through his mind, leaving his place of birth and migrating to an unknown country at the relatively young age of 22!

I was glad to hear that he had proved his worth in a career spanning almost 40 years in the East African nation. He was now retired and, after the founder's demise, had accepted the painful choice of relocating to India.

What I could comprehend after about ten minutes of our three-hour-long conversation was his prevailing sense of gratitude for the group and its founder. It is worth mentioning that the group's strong business ethics had instilled in him a sense of loyalty and integrity, and that he had great love for the people of this vibrant and peaceful country and their culture.

The gentleman, in his wisdom, offered to share his insights about the prevailing work culture that he had been exposed to. Before that, he shed some light on the family that ran the group and mentioned that the founder's four sons had called him over for a meeting a week before his departure to India. The siblings had asked him how much it would cost them to buy a plush three-bedroom house for a friend in India.

A day before his departure, the late founder's sons called on the gentleman and presented him, to his surprise, with an envelope. In it was a cheque equivalent to the value of a plush three-bedroom house in his hometown. I not only sensed the sheer gratitude of the founder but also understood that the founder had imparted high values to his children.

Before continuing with this part of his narrative, the gentleman briefed me about my meeting the following day with the founder's young grandson, whom he had dotingly held as a newborn.

Returning to his valuable insights, the gentleman cautioned me about the fact that I was stepping into untested waters and needed to be incredibly careful where I was going, especially while dealing with the lower-rung officials within the organisation. He also mentioned these people would go to lengths to break my resolve if I did not accede to their terms.

While reliving memories of the times he had spent at the founder's bungalow, the gentleman went on to describe how the colonel, a war veteran, spoke about the vast experience he had gained in three continents during the Second World War. He said the colonel was very articulate about a particular lesson that he made it a point to share with people of younger generations, along with what he had learnt during the wars he fought. The colonel also tended to add, *'I really liked Indians and learnt a lot about life's lessons from them. There are three things I came to realise from the wars I fought in India, Africa and Europe.'* The gentleman told me in a profound manner to keep these lessons in mind, especially for the meeting I was to have the next day.

He went on to talk about the colonel's three most significant lessons:

1. German secrecy.
2. British diplomacy.
3. Indian jealousy.

During the war, the Germans were developing atomic weapons, and the rest of the world had no inkling that they were doing so. The Allied Powers did not have a clue about Germany's nuclear capability. Such was the clandestine nature of Germans that it emboldened them on the frontlines. Many deemed it one of the greatest covert operations of the century!

Regarding the British, the colonel had learnt that they would easily buy time in any war just to make up for any gap in capability. What he was driving towards was that they were highly diplomatic in their war dealings and that one should doff one's hat to them for their finesse. He would speak of how Brits, across the ages, came and talked to the Indian maharajas or the Japanese imperials only to stab them in the back. British diplomacy was such that you would never know what they were up to—until you realised you were overrun.

And finally, the colonel said that one could break a kingdom overnight by pitting two brothers against each other and how Indians would fall for it. Indians were so jealous of each other that they would believe anything others said. He loved everything about Indians and India except for their jealousy. He called it 'the Indian jealousy'; the infamous Indian jealousy, just like the proverbial crabs in a bucket, with rivalry pervading all spheres of life, was out there for all to see. In his own strategic manner, the gentleman was cautioning me about the necessary working relationships that I would perhaps have to cultivate with Indians during my time in Africa.

This was something that hit close to home, as my father also spoke of how jealousy still prevailed in the world. I connected what the gentleman was telling with my father's history in business, thinking of the many people who were bestowed with his trust but deserted him and spoke unfavourably of his integrity and commitment. I also thought of how he had overcome all those challenges with sheer perseverance and dedication. Over the years, not only did my father learn the art of judging covetous people, but with time he went on to build a reputation where deceivers could no longer torment him.

While thinking about my father's life and words, I came to realise that dedication and perseverance allowed one to find the light at the end of the tunnel. I also understood that a person of good soul who fervently believed in their own inner strength and endured challenges unperturbed could not be pummelled by others.

I'm sure many of you think of giving up on many occasions during your journey but bear in mind that when you notice rocky shorelines, there is always this beacon of light to guide you. You just need to keep an eye out.

As our interaction ended, the gentleman asked if he could take his leave for the day and wished me the absolute best for my meeting the next morning. It was a very humble gesture of a well-wisher to have taken the time to say hello and prepare me for the road ahead.

The next morning, a hard-top Land Rover entered the hotel to pick me up. Its African driver greeted me with a pleasant smile and a loud '*Jambo!*' After an hour's drive, we reached the local factory where I was to experience the next affirmation.

Taking the Bull by Its Horns

Play by the rules but be ferocious.

Phil Knight

During the hour-long drive, I reflected on some of the valuable insights the Indian gentleman had shared with me the previous evening. What he said resonated well with what my father had cautioned me about! While I was still in deep thought, my driver manoeuvred the speeding car on a sharp bend, getting us to the entrance of a large factory. The noise of the equipment and machinery there was quite deafening. As I alighted from the car, a young well-groomed woman with an impeccable fashion sense and taste for clothes greeted me at the entrance of an old building and ushered me to the lobby. She introduced herself as the personal secretary to the Managing Director and requested me to cool my heels while offering me a cup of their signature coffee. After about 30-odd minutes, I was asked to proceed upstairs to meet the head of the company—a fine young lad.

Upon entering his plush cabin, a first glance displayed the youngster with finely chiselled features. He gazed intently at me, while I took sight of his dark, piercing eyes. Beneath his enigmatic yet warm smile was his trademark pompadour salt and pepper beard that gave him the appearance of a man much older for his age. Wearing his unique crisp white shirt, I caught a whiff of his tangy musk perfume that lingered across the hallway. Standing up to welcome me from his opulent sports car-themed luxury chair, I noticed that he was not just a tall man but an avid racing car enthusiast. Extending both his arms to greet me, I wished him with a firm handshake, while noticing his wristwatch, a timeless masterpiece.

He was in his mid-30s and everything the Indian gentleman had described to me. Having seen a picture of his grandfather during the previous day's discussions, I could tell there was a strong resemblance in the young lad; magnanimous and humble in every sense. He not only inherited the looks but also bore his grandfather's traits, especially humility and generosity that were an inherent part of his simple yet remarkable character.

The meeting with the young baron concluded on a positive note. As we exited the cabin, I could sense a wave of hostile emotions emanating from a few disgruntled staff members.

I went on to meet several officials and realised I could easily relate to what my father had been telling me all along about jealousy reigning among people, especially when you surpassed the lower rung of officials and directly built a relationship with the top brass. From their reactions, I sensed that I had pleased the king by ignoring his courtiers. I was indeed sure to land in trouble at some stage during my association with the conglomerate.

Coming back to business, the meeting with the young managing director was fruitful, and I went on to bag my first contract with the prestigious group despite the stiff resistance by despicable officials who tried to place unreasonable demands on my products and, by extension, to sully my image in the eyes of the management. These lower-order men had a penchant for defaming vendors who were not towing their line and engaged in shenanigans in broad daylight. I found it hard to fathom how such an approach had survived in an organisation built on such strong principles.

The first project was executed successfully soon enough; however, my happiness was short-lived, as I experienced my first brush with venality. I went ahead without conceding a dime to their demands.

The quality of the execution of the initial order was above everyone's expectations, and the young managing director and his father—who was the chairman—were both appreciative of my efforts. However, a certain clique within the organisation ensured that whenever I took a step forward, they would push me two steps backwards on the sly. Nevertheless, I didn't relent and began to get back-to-back orders. That was when the problems became unsurmountable; the coterie decided to target me by switching my high-quality product material with another local supplier's substandard material, thereby negatively impacting my future prospects with that company. They further went on to complain to the top brass that I was supplying inferior material that could pose a big risk to the plant's operations, something their management was unwilling to compromise on. All these unscrupulous activities were done in my absence and the absence of my site supervisors, leaving me without the choice to deal with the issue one-on-one.

Before I could even comprehend all that had happened, I was taken aback and appalled by the young managing director's callousness in not realising that a vendor of my repute would not tread the wrong path; he did not confront me with any evidence that I could have proved false. I was oblivious to how cut-throat businesses were, even for a reputed firm like mine which values its business ethics.

Prior to the false allegations against me and my company, I had visited the conglomerate once again to survey the plant and offer insights into their latest project which was vying around the corner. My subsequent presentation convinced the young managing director and his team to build a world-class packaging system. I returned home assuming it had been another successful trip. However, my happiness was short-lived as the contract that I was expecting never came through.

I tried connecting first with the lower-rung officials, who ignored me outright, and subsequently with my adviser friend in the conglomerate, who also left my calls and emails unanswered. Finally, with no option left, I tried connecting with the young managing director which left me exasperated, as I was ignored yet again. This fallout meant that something was amiss, and I realised that someone could have played maligner. I was later told that the contract had been awarded to a dubious vendor.

I narrated this to my father, and he shared an interesting anecdote about crabs in a bucket. We have all heard it so often. The thought he shared in connection with it gave the proverb a new dimension. The proverb itself refers to the behaviour of crabs. Whenever you have a bunch of crabs in a vessel and one of them tries to escape, the others will pull it down. This behaviour is seen in humans, too, particularly within a business landscape, more often than we would expect. It reflects the attitude that, '*If I can't have it, neither can you.*' When others see you advancing in life, their first instinct is often to discourage you or pull you down no matter what!

If only the crabs in the vessel worked together, they would all escape but, instead, they allowed selfishness and envy to destroy their chances. The same goes for human beings. Many of us want to be successful but are unwilling to help another person climb up the ladder unless we get something in return. Had the lower-rung officials been ethical in their dealings with me, I would have gone on to execute the project, and all the stakeholders could have benefited from the result. Ironically, the events that unfolded turned out just like what my father described in his narrative.

When someone you know is trying to do something remarkable or out of the ordinary, what is your gut reaction? For most of us, it is jealousy. But some of us have realised that helping others is how we get the things we want, too. We know that we can be smarter, better, and more cooperative than crabs. If you plan to climb out of your bucket, whatever the challenge may be, don't let others drag you down! If you are happy with what you've got but see a person going for something bigger, please give them a boost. Yes, you can do that much! It is indeed plausible that the reason the richest 10% of the world own and control so much is because they have embraced the culture of supporting one another. Meanwhile, the rest of the world continues to act like crabs in a bucket. Just like the legendary investor Warren Buffet once said, "*it is wise for investors to be 'fearful when others are greedy, and greedy when others are fearful'*.

With no solution in sight, I decided to ignore the problem at first and thought it was wise to give it some time. I then shifted gears, going back and taking hold of other emerging business opportunities in the African region that was fast becoming my second home. The next chapter goes on to reveal how, when my world was mentally falling apart due to the trials with the conglomerate, I went on to learn another of my father's greatest affirmations, which I will dwell upon at length.

To continue from where I left off, I learnt the ropes, earned my spurs, became aware of how to avoid similar pitfalls, and essentially resolved to fight it out on a not-so-level playing field. Not that the problems disappeared; I just learnt to deal with them ethically. From then on, I decided never to let a good challenge go to waste. Challenges refine you, mould you, and sharpen your intellect.

One early morning, as I was walking to my chambers, I noticed the first flowers blooming on the temple tree that was planted by the young managing director who had paid me a visit during one of his business trips. I had then made sure that he planted a tree as a tribute to his late grandfather, whom I revered from all that I had heard of him. Without thinking twice, I snapped a picture of the blooming yellow flowers and sent it across to the young baron. To my surprise, he replied with a touching note saying it was indeed a blessing from his grandfather in heaven. He further went on to enquire if I was doing well. His reply had made my day, as I was relieved from the inhibitions I had earlier. It felt like a heavy burden lifted off my chest. Symbolically, the blooming of the tree was like a renewed beginning for me and the African conglomerate.

A couple of days later, I received a call from my adviser friend in the group, asking me to inquire about a particular firm that, according to him, was my competitor. I denied having any knowledge of such a vendor who could be my close contender. I was asked to find out about the vendor's position in the industry and the authenticity of the claim regarding the same. I requested a couple of days' time to get back to the adviser on this.

After a thorough recce of the supplier, I informed the adviser that there was a possibility they were being conned, as the supplier had a bad reputation in the country. I was appalled, yet again, by the decision of the conglomerate to hand over to someone else the project that I had originally envisaged for the group, that too at a price higher than mine.

During the following week, just as I had intuited, the conglomerate came to realise that they had been duped, and I was immediately asked to fly over to meet the adviser and give them my opinion on whether the half-baked product supplied by the spurious vendor could still be put to use; the rest of the project was to be completed by me.

Upon my arrival, I quickly got out of the hard-top and dashed to the site location. To my despair, the incomplete supplies that had been provided by the fraudulent supplier were beyond reuse or rectification. I later realised that the top officials in the firm were sure that there was nothing they could salvage from this quagmire of their own making. Nevertheless, I began to understand that my presence was an excuse to award me another contract, which they were reluctant to have mentioned to me prior to my trip.

A couple of days later, the young baron called me over to his cabin and confided that he wasn't in the right frame of mind, while feigning ignorance of my fervent pleas for feedback on the status of the failed contract that had been awarded to my rival.

The owner of the African company went on to renew our business relationship. So much for people trying to pull me down! To me, the manner in which I cornered those lower-rung officials by judging them right was a vindication of sorts, and that learning came from the lesson my father had instilled in me—*take the bull by its horns*, by which he meant not just to fight the bull but to learn to tame it and eventually ride it!

First things first. Lesson number one—good business ethics will naturally bring in great business, no matter what.

Fight it!!!

During the prolonged meet in his cabin, although I was at risk of losing another huge prospect, I went ahead and gave the young baron my frank opinion, which was that it was unwise to go ahead with the half-baked product. He appreciated my honest feedback and stated that I had correctly judged the situation and analysed the outcome, although it was not pleasant for him to hear that from me. I revealed to him all that I was privy to about the contract.

Tame it!!!

He was taken aback by my straightforward and no-nonsense approach during our highly engaging discussions. I once again reminded him of the series of lapses on the part of the General Manager and his coterie. This, in turn, led to the sacking of the exposed General Manager who I believe had played a very venal role in awarding the dubious contract. It was at this very moment that the young baron realised his folly and resolved never to trust his officials without reason, something I realised over the course of my future business deals with the young lad.

Ride It!!!

With this, I broke the hold that the lower-rung officials had over the youngster. He saw reason and admired my ability to speak my mind without fear or favour. Never again did these officials resort to harassment of vendors, especially with me. I further ensured that their vicious intent would never drip into an organisation like mine that is deep-rooted in values and business ethics. Indeed, I had learnt to put a stop to their malicious allegations once and for all.

In a world that celebrates triumphant leaders and successful businessmen, like they are matadors in a bullfighting arena, many are unaware of the nitty-gritties of the fight. The business world too throws up quite a few similarities. A matador will tell you that every time he steps into the arena to take on a bull, it is a matter of life and death. There is both fear and respect for the charging bull, just as in the business world, which is no different, with numerous challenges being thrown at us each day.

Bullfighting is a sport that is widely held in awe for the valour of those who indulge in it; it is not for the squeamish. The business world, too, carries its own share of risks for those who play the game. However, the successful few who make it conceal their scars beneath their courage and their zeal to bring about a change in their world.

Watching my father closely, I've come to realise that building a business isn't everyone's cup of tea. It takes not just immense capital but years of effort to make an idea work. And that my father did through sheer grit and determination, by taking many bulls by their horns!

I have now learnt to meet challenges head-on, without cowing down to any unreasonable demands. This brings us to the end of one eventful experience and the beginning of another topic—lending a helping hand, which I will dive deep into.

***

A Good Deed Never Goes in Vain

Your greatness is not what you have,
it's what you give.

Alice Hocker

Like every business, mine too went through an upheaval with the African conglomerate as they moved slowly on their expansion plans, and some of their diversification strategies failed to bear fruit. I then decided to head over to meet a friend of mine in the 'City of Gold', not too far from East Africa.

A couple of hours into the flight, I reached the vibrant city of Johannesburg, and a further hour's drive got me to one of the most opulent parts of the city—Sandton in the Central Business District. Later that evening, my friend, who was a distributor of a leading product in an industry that I cater to, came over to meet me, following which we headed for dinner. He mentioned that my visit to Sandton would be incomplete without tasting steaks from the local steak house, to which I nonchalantly responded, *'Are they anywhere close to Australian steaks?'*

My friend was a bit taken aback by my query and made sure I gorged on a heavy steak to prove his claim, even though I was planning to go light on dinner. Little did I know I was treading into uncharted territory, and believe me, it's best not to get caught between these two former colonies—especially when it comes to their steaks, beer, or the love for the sport of rugby! I brooded over my off-the-cuff remark on the local steak as I dragged my stuffed belly to my hotel room, while also thinking of my future business prospects, which my South African friend told me about during our animated discussion over dinner.

The next day, I headed back to East Africa and scheduled a meet with the contacts my South African friend had recommended. Driving through the suburban townships, I reached the factory to meet my next prospect. It wasn't an ideal location for the main office of an African conglomerate. Nevertheless, I decided not to judge the book by its cover. After a few hours of waiting, I went on to meet my client's representative for a presentation on my products and capabilities. They were quite impressed with my presentation and were even more surprised about having been unaware of my product even though many of my competitors were already part of their vendor list. Blame it on our tame marketing outreach!

Over lunch at their premises, I couldn't hold on to my curiosity about an Indian gentleman who had noticed my arrival and, in turn, inquired about my presence. The representative of the firm informed me that he was the owner of the group. This made me even more inquisitive, and I asked about his conglomerate and its diverse portfolios. I was startled to know how the owner, a noble temple priest from India, had come down to East Africa to manage the affairs of a temple and worked part-time to make ends meet. When he was rendered jobless, even a day's meal was unaffordable for him. As luck would have it, he got a chance at redemption and started a small trading firm, which was a stepping stone to the formation of a successful enterprise. Under his leadership, the group went on to become one of East Africa's most reputed firms, with one foot in business and the other firmly in their charitable deeds.

It was at this very moment that another of my father's greatest affirmations came to my mind when I heard that the well-settled former temple priest had pledged more than half of his multi-million-dollar fortune to the welfare of the people of the East African nation. I could relate this to the attitude of my father, who would always correct me when I questioned his charitable work, especially when we were in dire straits. His feeble reply was always: *'It's more blessed to give than to receive. When you give to someone who is worthy of your help, nature gives it back manifold, especially when you need it the most.'* He went on to further reveal how, on many occasions, our organisation could have collapsed, but help always came in at the right time.

In a way, I could relate it to my father's humble beginnings and hardships, that he faced during his childhood days and how on many occasions he was extricated from his deprivations of day-to-day necessities when help came in the least expected manner, which in turn was a stimulus for his charitable nature. In a way, he would always attribute his success to his mother who had always extended a helping hand to those in need despite their limited means.

The key takeaway from this experience is that charity is very important in one's life. Though I had only heard of people talking about charity, I had never experienced the act of genuinely giving, let alone that of receiving a favour in return, particularly when I needed it the most. The rest of this chapter takes you through one of the most momentous phases of my life, during which I experienced that when you offer help to a person in need, nature finds a way of giving it back, particularly when you are down and out.

My meeting with the new East African conglomerate went successfully, culminating in a contract. On my way back home, I flew to the Pearl of the Indian Ocean—Sri Lanka—for a visit to one of my ongoing project sites. After a quick immigration process at the cramped arrival centre, I headed to a plush hotel not far from the airport. I was famished and went straight to bed only to be awakened by the chirping of birds amidst the dense vegetation the hotel was nestled in.

I had a penchant for confessing to a Catholic priest every weekend, which had been a custom of mine since my childhood. I inquired about it at the hotel reception and was directed to the nearest church, which was surprisingly a short walk from my hotel. On reaching the church, I found the only priest of the parish celebrating the Holy Mass, and soon after, he dashed to his quarters. I was quite disappointed that I missed seeing him leave from the sacristy. I stayed on for a while, only to be informed by the deacon that the priest would be available to meet guests only after five that evening. I decided to get back to the hotel for a sumptuous breakfast and proceed onward to my project site.

As I reached the construction site, which was equidistant from my hotel and the church, I realised we were far behind the commissioning schedule, with the planned date to commence production fast approaching. I couldn't believe that, though we had left no stone unturned, nothing was going in our favour. I was further taken aback when I got to know that government officials had declined work permits to a few of my supervisory colleagues who were supposed to work at the project site for longer durations—this refusal diminished the chances of us completing the project on schedule, forget about the risks it entailed, given that the piece of equipment we were setting up was one of the largest of its kind in the Indian subcontinent.

My supervisory staff were most important to me, and I could hardly imagine staying back myself to supervise all the complex, painstaking, risky protocols involved in their absence. Tired as I was amidst the humid conditions and the lack of direction on the work front, I decided to take a break before my night shift workers arrived. It was indeed important for me to meet the shift managers, discuss handing over protocols and strategise a plan to accelerate the work.

While I wanted to head over to the hotel and rest for a couple of hours, my intuition prompted me to head back to the church and meet the priest for a confession.

Upon getting there, I saw the priest with his cassock folded, riding pillion on a bike. Noticing me, he waved and asked me to follow him. I was desperately in need of divine intervention, consumed by the concern that the slow progress of work and the day-to-day obstacles that I faced could be attributed to my having displeased God by not fulfilling my promise to confess to a priest on a weekly basis.

Not wanting to lose the opportunity, I ran behind the priest with my cab driver following me, which was reminiscent of a scene from a comedy movie that I had watched recently. I quickly realised I wouldn't be able to catch up with the priest and decided to get into my cab, vaguely following the priest through busy Colombo dwellings.

A while later, the cab reached a narrow road. There was no trace of the bike or the priest. Just then, I heard a bell ring and realised there was another church nearby. I quickly walked towards the bell tower and saw the humble priest sweeping the nearby trash-riddled alleyway.

The priest, noting that I had probably had a tiresome day, offered me some lemonade brought by one of the local parishioners. Seeing me gulp down the drink, he smiled and quickly ushered me to a nearby tree that had two chairs under it.

Following a good confession, we headed towards an under-construction building within the church premises whose site was strewn with garbage; the church was situated near a garbage dump. The land was quite fertile due to the low-lying terrain that it was situated in, and the priest quickly walked me around, mentioning that it was his long-standing dream to have the marshland cleaned up and the construction work completed during his tenure. The place, despite all the trash, was beautiful and serene, interspersed with lakes and lagoons.

I was also informed that the facility would serve as a makeshift relief centre during floods or as a coaching centre for underprivileged students. It was indeed a humongous task to have the place cleaned up, even with the wholehearted support of the locals.

A couple of strides later, I noticed that, though the under-construction skeletal building was almost complete, the main entrance lacked a roof over it. I inquired with the priest about how he planned to construct a massive roof on a building that looked frail and was probably not designed to withstand the load of the roof.

The priest was at his wits end on how to proceed. He told me that the young engineer who had designed the place did not realise his folly until the building was ready for a roof. I swiftly suggested that the only solution was to have a lightweight steel structure over it. The priest found merit in what I had suggested and inquired about how much it would cost to complete the roof. My response shocked the priest: *'Nothing less than a million rupees!'*

The priest was uncertain of diocesan support for this, as he had already approached them for out-of-the-way assistance on more than one occasion. It was very painful to see the priest's earnest desire—to complete the makeshift centre so that the local populace could make good use of it—go unfulfilled.

I bid goodbye to the priest. On my way back to the car, my intuition prompted me to offer a helping hand in building the roof. It was, after all, my forte—I was a trained structural engineer myself.

I walked back to the priest and offered to help him complete his long-awaited dream. There were tears of joy in his eyes, and a firm handshake followed. For the priest, it was the end of a long-drawn battle, while for me, it was just the beginning of a long path.

After I conducted a deeper analysis of the building, the problems began to mount in quick succession. Firstly, the pillars were much more fragile than I had imagined, and they lacked certain inherent connections without which they would not be able to hold a roof.

Next, I realised that most of the raw materials required to build the roof had to be imported from India or China, as the locally available sections were just not suited to this application. I quickly told him that I had some consignments that were yet to be dispatched from my facility and that, once I got back home, I would work on a proposal and send it to him.

It was getting dark. I went back to the project site to begin another week of despair on the work front. There was nothing I could do, as the most basic needs of the hour were my human assets—skilled supervisors, to whom the local government was not keen on issuing work permits due to strict labour laws.

I indeed needed a miracle of sorts to take on the challenges that lay ahead and face my client, who was in no mood to relent on the completion date. I could understand my client's desperation, as he needed to start production to repay the huge loans he had taken. The revisions of the project commissioning date on various occasions due to reasons other than those related to my product further worried the management. The last thing I wanted was another extension in the inaugural date, which would have huge financial repercussions on us all.

Every day was a challenge until one fine morning when I noticed the priest walking by the project site. A few of my co-workers insisted that I request the priest to bless the under-construction facility, to which he readily agreed. The entire workforce, including the plant owners, who were Buddhists, joined the prayer and blessing session. The priest went on to touch my senses when he said, '*Son, when you have gone out of your way to assist us with the shelter home, rest assured that help will certainly arrive from unexpected quarters.*' Having relieved me of my anxieties regarding another delay in the completion date, the priest bid us goodbye.

After a tiring week at the site, I headed back to my country to review the manufacturing status of the pending consignments, as the Sri Lankan project was becoming a race against time. I also used this opportunity to work on the makeshift shelter home for the church and have it delivered before my project completion in Sri Lanka.

With the priest having reviewed and approved the drawings, I wasted no time in having the steel roof fabricated. After about a month, we had the roof delivered as a knock-down unit to the parish in Colombo.

My subsequent visit to Sri Lanka for the site review was followed by a visit to the church. I was greeted by the local community and witnessed their gratitude. Before settling down amidst all the praise, the priest and I faced our next big upheaval when we realised the structure needed to be assembled with the help of a crane, and large pieces of equipment were needed to mount it on the under-construction makeshift centre. The path leading to the makeshift centre was extremely narrow, and, with my busy schedule, I had no choice but to abandon the work and leave it to the helpless priest and the locals to find a way out. I then headed back to my project site.

I entered the site office to my supervisors ecstatically singing praises of the Almighty, as a group of highly skilled migrant Sri Lankan labourers had just returned to their homeland for good. They had completed a long and arduous work contract in the Middle East. Having heard about our contribution to the local church, these men were willing to help us at the project site as a goodwill gesture, knowing very well the challenges that were at hand.

These ironworkers had elevated levels of expertise in erecting large steel structures and were willing to help us surpass our most significant challenge, which was to mount one of the largest grid beams ever erected in the Indian subcontinent. They were also keen to start work with the local contractors immediately, which was a blessing in disguise.

I realised how one of my father's greatest affirmations had worked out for me; providence had found its way of helping me in return for a good deed that I had just done.

As I was leaving the project site, the head of the newly appointed labourers' group came over to me and offered to help us with erecting the makeshift centre of the church, as he too was part of the same parish.

Overwhelmed and twice lucky! I was previously worried about how I would have to divert the workforce from the already overburdened project site to erect the roof at the makeshift centre, considering the lack of a skilled workforce and the fast-approaching deadline.

The next morning, I received a call from the priest, who requested me to visit the makeshift centre. As I made my way there, I noticed that the locals had widened the path by filling soil over the lagoons in a bid to allow the crane to access the makeshift centre.

I was humbled by the down-to-earth locals, to whom the parish and the makeshift centre meant everything. Never had I seen such unity and dedication from a local community. I returned to the project site to review the situation and formulate a plan to hire mobile cranes for the erection of the grid beams.

Later that evening, the owner of the project site and I left to meet the crane service provider, as the crane hiring was under the ambit of the plant owner. Upon reaching the office of the service provider, we were astonished to learn that the only such crane available in the whole of Sri Lanka had been diverted to another site due to our delay in positioning the grid beams at their desired location prior to its erection.

The plant owner was heartbroken, as we would have to delay the project by over a week, and I would be forced to make up for the lost time.

The service provider, who was aware of my virtuous deeds at the makeshift centre, was willing to risk his contractual obligations by mobilising the crane to our project site. He went a step ahead and again offered to help us with more equipment to erect the roof structure, that too free of cost.

In fact, the story of a foreigner offering to build the roof over the makeshift centre had spread like wildfire in the local community.

A couple of months later, the country's largest fabricated silo was erected, and so was the roof over the makeshift centre. For me, it added not one but two feathers to my hat. Having completed the project, I bid goodbye to all the workmen and the plant owner before returning to my country and to my routine of coming up with new marketing strategies and focusing on my company's expansion.

Soon, however, I received a call from the priest. He informed me that the story of the makeshift centre had made it to the cardinal, and the locals insisted that I be felicitated at the inauguration of the centre. I was humbled yet again by the locals, who never forgot to value a person from whom they had received favours. Well, from my experience, all it takes is one small gesture to show you care, and society repays you with an overwhelming rush of gratitude and blessings. Many were inspired by my intention of going out of my way to help the underprivileged; well, it was I who drew inspiration from my father for another of his key affirmations, and from the Sri Lankan locals, for their stoicism and sheer determination in contributing to the well-being of society.

I was invited by the priest and the locals, who requested me to bring my family along for the celebrations, which were to be presided over by the cardinal himself. The following month, I headed to the island nation yet again, but this time as a tourist, to revisit another of my father's affirmations—lending a helping hand.

After the celebrations, which involved over 2,000 locals, I was felicitated with a memento and a letter from the priest in the presence of the cardinal, His Eminence Albert Malcolm.

The letter read:

"It's more blessed to give than to receive.

The best way if you want your money to flow according to your conscience is to help in charitable work.

What matters is not the quantity but the intention.

Donation is a sign of solidarity, unity, and cooperation.

Religion cannot exist without kindness and contribution. Your donation reflects on you, and it gives relief to your mind. It further gives you a feeling that you do something for the world that you live in.

When you donate, you receive more than you expect.

Giving is more about quality values than quantity.

Giving is more a blessing than an obligation. Your wealth becomes stronger when you contribute to worthy causes than making more and more.

It is better to measure life by its donations than its duration."

***

Truth & Lust

Lust should be stifled, for it cannot lead to truth.

Moses Ibn Ezra

Another interesting event that transpired in Africa yielded insights into a specific person's character. One evening, as we concluded a critical discussion about an upcoming greenfield project with the conglomerate, I could sense a tense atmosphere brewing around its senior manager and his cohort as we arrived at a seemingly impossible solution. A few business acquaintances and I, who were part of the discussion, decided to call it a day and headed to a nearby downtown restaurant for dinner.

Just as we settled into the large dining area, the high-pitched officials, along with their senior manager, surprisingly took a nearby table. Their character seemed prodigal and a total contrast to the ambience. Suddenly, an argument broke out at their table over the behaviour of the senior manager and his friends with a good-looking woman who was serving them. The young woman rebuffed the vile and cowardly acts. While on her way to the kitchen, she paused midway and, gathering all her wits, lambasted the officials for their unruly behaviour, much to the perceptible gasps from the be-sequined guests. The youngster further threatened to lodge a formal complaint with the local authorities, while the cohort, unstirred, retaliated with further abuses and threatened her, insinuating that none of her threats would have an effect nor stall their frequent transgressions and ulterior motives.

It was at this moment that I realised these officials were frequent visitors to the restaurant who tormented the youngster by intimidation. These men were ranting on and a domineering bunch of bullies. I was immensely surprised that a couple of officials at my table too were complicit in the events that unfolded with the youngster.

While I chastised the officials at my table, I was speechless when they responded that these were the brutal realities for a woman working late in a restaurant, that too in the 21st century.

Well, for people like me, these acts of chauvinism were seen as an adroit cudgel to get intimate in the guise of whining about the quality of her service and her demeaning attitude.

Call it naïveté, but my gut feeling further reinforced my belief that the senior manager's baser instincts appeared to have taken over, and he was coming onto her rather abusively. His disposition and demeanour spoke volumes about his character. I impulsively once again shared my thoughts with my business acquaintances at the table. I told them that I could almost see the lust in him.

My father always used to say that two things should be kept at extremes from each other:

- One should relate truth to virtue and have more of it.
- One should relate lust to iniquity and have the least of it.

Lust is nothing but an excess of desire. One tends to get consumed by lust when one does not know how to limit one's boundaries or stifle one's desires. This vice, if left unchecked, goes on to reach another realm called gratification, which sadly is the point of no return. Lust is not necessarily for sexual pleasure; it could also be for power or take the form of gluttony or other materialistic desires such as avarice.

While on the topic of lust, relationships come to the fore. For in lust, an individual looks to the opposite sex as a commodity instead of acknowledging the beauty of another individual's soul. Lust is fundamentally an inexplicable problem that inflicts incalculable suffering on lives, families, and relationships.

My father saw three ways of expressing lustful behaviour: through a person's eyes, body, and conduct. As the adage goes, '*The eyes say it all.*' The gaze of a person is one of the most revealing signs of their lust. Both men and women tend to fixate visually on a person's body for a prolonged duration or repeatedly, oblivious to their surroundings. At the same time, while being fixated on a person's physical attributes, they seem to be lost in a euphoric world, not realising how they are giving themselves away.

Similarly, body language is another sign of a person overtly using the body to make an undeniable statement of lustful intent, be it through physical touch, an open stance, or a sexual gesture.

Finally, a person's conduct speaks volumes about their intentions, especially when a man behaves intimidatingly with the fairer sex. He further elucidated that it is best to distance oneself from such iniquitous men and women, who would go to any lengths to break one's character for their very own personal gains. These are the same people who lack the morals and virtues to lead an honest private and public life, and it is best to have their inherent traits under check, especially while dealing with them.

On my next trip to Africa, I came to know that an innocent executive in the African conglomerate was made the fall guy in a major sexual scandal involving the senior manager and his cohort, thereby losing his high-stakes job. Little did the executive realise when he engaged in his iniquitous behaviour that his lustful desires would go on to create a major upheaval in his life. Those who trapped him were his canny friends, who exploited his weakness and made the best of the situation. In other words, it takes one to know one.

In my case, my father's wise words on truth and lust ignited a passion in me to deeply understand how these traits have gone on to make or break empires.

As we dwell deeper on these qualities, they offer contrasting insights about a person. My father would relate truth to a person's 'character' and lust to their 'intention'. This was a startling revelation for me, and it became fundamental to my understanding of human behaviour. In hindsight, this gave me an edge in understanding people and their ulterior motives.

Moving onto the subject of truth, my father always believed that truth was not a property of thoughts and ideas, but more of beliefs and assertions. For him, truth was all about winning another person's trust. I began to understand from him that truth was constructive and rewarding, while lies were destructive and punitive.

So how beneficial have these thoughts or reactions been for me? Am I just covering up an irrational fear or helping to create a solid foundation for the future? Am I empowering myself to fulfil my highest potential or depriving myself of opportunities to enrich my life or create problems in the future? Will this cycle repeat itself, or will the truth at last set me free?

While some broad reflections on the above get me thinking about this great affirmation, I believe what my father did was lay a road map that gave me the answers which, in turn, led me to my destination with my head held high. In other words, what he taught me was to keep truth and lust at opposite extremes.

Truth is the bedrock of trust, and my father's life made me realise this. In fact, not only business alliances but even relationships fail due to trust deficits. My father's life has taught me to always give prominence to truth, thereby winning the trust of all.

As I saw it, there was a broken link between truth and trust. This got me to think more deeply about how easily and quickly my father went on to gain the trust of many business houses and societies during his lifetime. It was only during my visit to the local parish in this remote African town that I gained insights into this unsolved mystery.

The morning after the distressing event at the downtown restaurant, I decided to head to the local parish for the Sunday service. I had brought along with me some local savouries from my home country and decided to share them with the parishioners after the holy service. I was touched to see the gratitude in the eyes of many humble Africans who couldn't thank me enough, as foreigners very rarely brought them handmade sweets from their hometowns. A little while into the distribution, a gentleman came forward to help me. His was a familiar face, and on inquiring, I realised it was one of the local officials from the conglomerate who admired my passion for work and my courage in taking on the unscrupulous cohort at the firm on many occasions.

After the distribution, we went back to our bases until we met the subsequent week for a debate with the young Turk. While the cohort was very much against my equipment's performance, the local official from my Sunday meet vouched for my equipment's quality, much to the anguish of the cohort. I went on to gain the confidence of the young owner and bag my next deal.

Just after the meet, as I stepped outside, the local official walked up to me and, upon my inquiring about why he had risked his career to stand up for me, his reply took me by surprise. He said he too wished to be an altruist like me. Shaking hands and looking deeply into my eyes, he bid me goodbye.

It took me a while to realise what he was trying to convey. Well, it was clear that I had won his trust. Over time, this incident helped me realise that altruism was that missing link between truth and trust. In other words, it was innately my father's passion in everything he did, whether for a social cause or for a client, that went on to help us overcome our impediments.

It's all the more imperative for business houses to lay a strong emphasis on the crucial element of trust. To elaborate further, gaining the trust of all stakeholders, such as the board, the management team, the clients, and the employees, is of paramount importance to the establishment of an organisation's brand. Today, the trust quotient of a brand is valued as much within the organisation as it is from the outside.

Trust has come to mean different things to different people. While trust does vary culturally in magnitude, it is basically about one's credibility and integrity. However, truth precedes trust, and trust is the predecessor to a reciprocal bond, which is fundamental to human relationships. Altruism is the trait that cements such relationships, binding people and organisations together.

I have come to believe from my father's life that, unless there is truth and altruism, trust is impaired. And that leads to the precipitous end of one's journey to success. Because trust is the bedrock of success.

Plant a Tree

He who plants a tree, plants a hope.

Lucy Larcom

I managed to gain the firm trust of the young baron after skirmishes with lower-rung officials and an unexpected turn of events with the same conglomerate, which I will cover later in this book. Never did I realise my next trip would be life-changing—especially in terms of my relationship with nature.

It all began on a business trip to Singapore when I was at lunch with my client at a well-known restaurant in Little India overlooking the Rochor River. I was mesmerised by the neighbourhood, teeming with life and colour, especially the women, who were vivacious in traditional attire. Amidst these vivid surroundings, I was left speechless when I received a call from the office of the African conglomerate asking me to visit India for discussions with their Indian consultants and to negotiate a deal for their upcoming greenfield project in East Africa. All this while, I believed I was persona non grata in the conglomerate due to the recent events with their officials.

After completing the travel formalities, the next morning, I rushed to the airport for my flight to India, a country with a wealth of historic edifices and rich cultural heritage. A short flight from Singapore got me to a south Indian city the evening before the African opportunity meeting. This city was rich in tradition, with numerous temples, churches, mosques, and gurudwaras. Located along the coast, the city, with its alluring white sand beaches and lip-smacking seafood, is one of my favourite destinations in India—all the more so because I relished the onion dosa and powder chutney the city is famous for. I never missed the opportunity to have this scrumptious meal, especially while sipping piping hot filter coffee—the fragrance of chicory was pure bliss. The city was known for its vibrant life and ancient architecture—it had everything a traveller could want.

Much as I desired to head out for an evening stroll and to have my favourite dish, I had to deny myself that pleasure, since I had been invited for a hearty meal by a friend's brother, a fine young lad and a chef himself, with his own eatery. I called to check on him and was overwhelmed by the warmth in his voice, typifying the city's culture. He was awaiting my call, as his sister had informed him about my visit, and she wanted to ensure that he met me—which I later realised was a trick to have me deliver a package for her brother in India.

I grabbed my raincoat as it was pouring and quickly dashed to the hotel reception to catch an Uber. I learnt the city's traffic had gotten into a massive gridlock. The hotel receptionist informed me that the city was seeing protests due to some political instability, and that was why it had come to a grinding halt.

I was dismayed that I had to walk on such a rainy day. To my surprise, a rickshawala offered to drop me to my destination. Incidentally, it was the same tuk-tuk I had hired for a joyride during one of my previous trips, a humble soul with whom I'd had the privilege of sipping one of the traditional filter coffees the city is famous for. As I entered the rickshaw, he enlightened me about the massive crowd on the streets—a famous personality had been admitted to a nearby hospital, and it was customary in India to gather in large numbers and express solidarity for the personality who had been hospitalised. I would call it idolising and sycophancy, an attitude that was predominant in most parts of the developing world. He then quickly manoeuvred his rickshaw into the bylanes, criss-crossing through the locality and, within a few minutes, I got to a street close to my destination. The rickshawala dropped me off at the nearest point, as the rest of the street was cordoned off.

When I asked how much I owed him for the ride, he declined any fare as a sign of respect for the coffee I had bought him during one of my previous trips. I realised the city was full of people with generosity and warmth. As I alighted from the rickshaw and started walking towards the restaurant, which was at the end of the street, I saw Indian police officials in khaki and heard scores of sirens blaring all over.

While I was walking towards my destination, a senior woman officer stopped me and asked what I was doing at the cordoned-off junction. I replied that I was visiting a friend who lived down the street, and I showed her the location on the map. She initially denied me permission to head over to the restaurant as the protests were flaring up.

I quickly called up my friend, who said he would speak to the officer. They communicated in the local language, and I was permitted to visit his restaurant. The road had gotten extremely busy and crowded with police officers and high-profile individuals visiting the hospital, which was close to the restaurant that I was heading to.

As I reached the end of the street, a smiling face greeted me at the entrance of a large gate that was wide open. I was sure I had met my host. I was startled by all the commotion and politely inquired about what was going on. He too narrated the same story the receptionist and the rickshawala had told me.

With a few steps into his massive property, I again felt the calm and positive vibes this great cultural city was known for. I realised there were no security guards, and the gates weren't shut despite the cacophony of people, police, high-profile stars, and celebrities. When we reached the restaurant, I was startled yet again by every piece of art he had collected over the years, with each work a total contrast to the previous one.

He offered me his signature fruit punch and pan-fried momos. While sipping the welcome drink, I expressed curiosity about the woodwork around his restaurant. He replied that every piece of wood, including some of the outdoor furniture items, was made of the two trees he had had to fell because they were obstructing pedestrian movement to the hospital. I found this a bizarre reason to have had to fell the trees, given that the street did not even have a pedestrian pathway. It was, in fact, common for people in India to walk freely on the streets. I could sense the vengeance of the hospital authorities next door hiding behind the intrigue.

Anyway, I went on to ask him if I could see the entire property. He showed me around. The property was full of trees from almost every continent across the world, and I was astounded by his knowledge of them. His pride was the African baobab tree, which, despite being 20 years old, looked like a young tree. He also mentioned that he had only felled the two trees because he had had no choice, but he had made sure that every piece of wood that he could salvage was utilised to make artistic furniture, from wooden mushrooms to wall hangings.

He mentioned that he tended to every tree like it was family and emphasised that they were very much living beings. I felt the connection between him and trees. This was reminiscent of how my father would treat the trees he planted. I was also trying to connect this experience to my experience with a Spanish co-passenger who had also flown from Singapore to the south Indian city.

While it was natural for me to connect with strangers, especially during journeys, I must confess that some of the greatest lessons I've learnt in life have come from men and women whom I've met while travelling to various parts of the world. This journey, too, was no exception.

My latest co-traveller and I got into a conversation, thanks to his pleasant demeanour. This discussion veered around his nature and calm disposition. I was also a bit intrigued about the fragrance he was wearing and asked about it. He attributed it to 'the palo santo'.

'Palo Santo, is that a brand?' I asked.

His reply amused me. *'Haven't you heard of the holy wood?' he asked back.*

I was a bit surprised by how astounding it was to him that I did not know about 'the holy wood'. With a calm disposition, he explained how the wood—which is native to South America and widely used by the indigenous tribes and the shamans of the continent—was discovered centuries ago by Spanish monks who went on to baptise this mystical tree as the 'holy wood' or 'wood of the saints'.

The Incas and other indigenous tribes would smudge the oil and burn sticks from the tree for sacred rituals and healing. What caught my attention was the belief that the tree was home to a spirit. The tree was hence considered a living entity, strange as it may sound. Many civilisations around the world still believe in this concept of an inert being. The co-passenger added details about how the spirit continued dwelling in the tree long after it had fallen of its own accord.

Hence, the palo santo is never harvested. He told me that the healing properties and fragrances of the tree develop only when the tree is allowed to die a natural death, and the spirit in the tree is given its due respect.

Back to the restaurant. Before I could wet my tanned leather shoes any further in the unpruned lawns, my friend's brother and I quickly hurried back in where a small heater had been arranged for, as the city was cold after the steady deluge of rains. He offered me a nice warm cup of tea and, as I was sipping, I expressed some more curiosity, asking him how he had come to live on such a massive property all by himself without a single guard and with the gates wide open the whole time.

He told me that the property was the most expensive one in the city and he had been offered a hefty sum for it by a well-known personality who wanted to build a skyscraper on it—an offer he declined. The same person then sent a local lobby group that indirectly threatened him to get him to sell the property—threats he vehemently resisted. A week later, that same personality died of a sudden heart ailment.

This conversation was getting interesting.

His second brush with land sharks mirrored the first, with another famous personality sending his henchmen. Misfortune befell this personality, too—he was involved and exposed in a corruption scandal and then imprisoned. The story went on in this manner until a fifth personality asked him to sell his property for almost twice the initial price, an offer he refused yet again. He asked me to guess who the person was.

Just as I began connecting the dots, he whispered that the famous personality was the one admitted in hospital right now, just across the street.

Hence the cause for all the commotion.

The icing on the cake was his revelation that he stayed all alone on this property, which was peculiar for people living in India—especially so given that he lived without security and with his gates wide open, despite threats from land sharks looming large. I asked about this.

He said, '*Every single person who came to threaten and steal my property had this bad luck inflicted on them. I believe my trees are my greatest guardians, the seeds that God has planted to take care of people like me!*'

I was quite taken aback by this entire episode and recollected how my father had a similar love for trees. In fact, ours was one of those few industries where one of the trees served as shelter to people working below it. The branches of the tree grew out of an industrial shed and they provided shade to everything below. My father believed that we as humans had misused our rights and that it wasn't right for anyone to ever fell a tree unless there was an absolute need. He also earnestly wondered how good it would be if men and trees could co-exist.

The story of the restaurateur bore a stark resemblance to my father's life. He, too, dealt with threats on both the business and personal fronts, and his trees had always formed a protective shield around him. It would also be prudent here to reference the story of the Spaniard, who held on to his reverence for palo santo, a tree of such significance in South American folklore.

To date, no tree has ever been felled at our manufacturing facility. And the lesson—how trees stand tall as the ultimate custodians—has been absorbed by every employee at our organisation, with each of them pledging to make trees an integral part of their everyday life.

Many of us undermine the value of trees because of their inert nature—trees are the basis of our very existence and survival. Going by my personal experience, it wouldn't be too far-fetched to say that trees provide a protective atmosphere to people around them. This might sound fictitious, but drawing upon one of my closest brushes with the African conglomerate, I can still remember how I got out of that precarious situation and credited that miracle with the baobab tree, which they call 'the tree of life'.

One fine early morning, I took a walk around the savannah and came across a large baobab tree at the periphery of the factory. Just as I was about to cross the boundary, I noticed a tall African in his traditional attire holding a spear. I tensed up, as the man appeared belligerent. He smiled to indicate that he meant no harm—he probably realised I was surprised at his attire. I began to calm down.

Just then, a loud voice from the distant guest house caught our attention. It was Sammy, my chauffeur, who was waving and running towards us. As he got closer, I could make out that he was speaking in the local dialect, probably telling the African man that I was new to the countryside and unaware while treading the periphery of the factory that it was rife with thieves.

Sammy went on to introduce me to the local natives, called the Masai, and told me how the large factory was well-protected despite the lack of a fence around it and threats from local thieves. He lauded the loyalty and dedication of the local Masai, entrusted with taking care of the factory since many of the local policemen and security guards were fearful of the sinister local elements and unwilling to guarantee a theft-free facility. I wondered how the Masai braved the local intrusions, which had been rampant for years, and this wonderment stirred up a sense of concern in me—for their livelihoods and lives. At that very moment, the Masai grinned, almost like he got a whiff of what I was concerned about.

I asked Sammy if I could head over to the large baobab, as I had never seen such a gigantic tree. Sammy gleefully gave his assent and ushered me towards the tree. The Masai tribesman tagged along. As the three of us stood awestruck in front of the mighty tree, the Masai said something to Sammy, who translated and relayed to me that the Masai slept peacefully at night because the baobab watched over them and kept any negativity or evil at bay.

My father, the restaurateur, the Spaniard, and the Masai tribesman had not just seen it from an eco-conscious standpoint, but from within—how the Almighty has actually planted trees to serve and protect every living creature on this planet. The insularity of people today, especially in terms of understanding the significance of trees, has led not just to an ecological impact but a sense of apathy for the ones we hold close, unlike our true guardians—the trees—who have been there for us since the dawn of time.

That brings me to a rather new, interesting, and debatable topic—sexual austerity.

***

Sexual Austerity

Fire, after all, does not consume. It transmutes.

Kaia Anderson

Getting back to my hotel amidst all the hustle and bustle of the metropolitan, I retired to my bed thinking about the next morning's critical negotiations for the new project with the African conglomerate. My focus was fixated on how to convince the young baron that my company was a strong contender, as he could be misguided by the lower-rung officials who were accompanying him. Nevertheless, I steered my thoughts away from these considerations and went into a deep slumber.

The next morning, I headed for the meeting with an understanding that there were only four other bidders, but to my astonishment, I found out that there were 12! In fact, a few of these organisations were startups that were in the nascent stages of growth. I presumed the African owners had been tricked into believing that these 12 were reliable vendors by his advisers. However, in my opinion, they were neither reliable nor capable of handling a project of this magnitude.

As time passed, I grew worried because the scope of work had certain ambiguities that the unreliable vendors could use to their advantage by lowering their prices initially and going on to arm-twist the client for a price escalation at a later date—much to our disadvantage, as we had a reputation for never going back to a client with any such monetary claims once we had signed a covenant with a client.

Moving on to the project specifications, it was a worrying instance for me, particularly about the pricing strategy that I had to adopt since the plant machinery had to operate continuously 24/7 for almost a year with a maximum downtime of only up to 3 hours for any unforeseen events of breakdown. In other words, the system was to perform like a Mustang while being built like a Pinto with the cost constraints included.

Although we were the best bidders for the project, especially given the soundness of our technology, we were hardly given any importance during the 12-hour-long meeting, of which almost 11 hours were spent in solitude by me. I was made to wait while the other bidders were called for numerous rounds of negotiations.

It was my longest wait, and I was beginning to wonder if I would ever be called in for the negotiations. I also began to prepare myself for the worst, as this loss would spur my competitors to spread rumours of our decline as a preferred vendor in the market, especially in the East African region. Another intuitive feeling preying on my mind was the question of whether the baron was being tricked by the plant maintenance team in Africa into believing that our product performance was not up to the prevailing standards.

Cutting back to the project-bidding event, I was asked to proceed for dinner while the young baron and other bidders dashed to the dining area. Their disposition and demeanour were sardonic, as many were aware of our stature as one of the front runners in winning the bid. Considering our many decades of experience in the execution of such critical projects, our reputation preceded us. At the same time, our products were sophisticated and impenetrable.

Offended by the young baron feigning ignorance, I hastily finished my meal and scrambled towards the exit, agitated and deeply hurt. Just then, a loud voice called out my name from behind. As I turned around, to my astonishment, it was the young baron who strode towards me. On reaching, he extended his customary greeting, a firm handshake, and an exuberant hug, much to the dismay of my competitors.

It was almost half-past 11 at night when I hurried to take the red-eye back home. I had to speed through the city's traffic to get to the airport to make it for another important milestone in my life, the inauguration of a new production facility we had set up as a tribute to my father. But, as not everything is in our hands, I missed my flight. I was devastated that I would miss the inauguration and one of the greatest moments of my life the next morning. Alas! I had missed the last flight, and there was no way I could get back home in time. But God probably had other plans.

Suddenly, an elderly woman from another airline, who was witnessing my distress, inquired if I wanted to head back to my destination and elucidated that the previous flight to my city had been delayed, and she could help me get a ticket to board the flight, which would surprisingly leave in half an hour. She went on to add it was totally up to the pilot, who could accommodate me as an exception.

A short while later, the woman walked up to me and said the pilot had obliged, quipping that we had to get to the flight in under five minutes. She immediately arranged for someone to usher me to the boarding gate and security check; thankfully, I made it just in time.

As I settled down in my seat, with the flight yet to be cleared for take-off due to the sudden incessant rains, I chanced upon the opportunity and narrated all that had transpired during the long arduous meeting to my father, including the news of us having bagged the deal at the last minute. Just then, an elderly passenger beside me who had overheard my discussion with my father started a conversation. The intrigued passenger inquired about my day-long ordeal and how I had bagged the deal. The co-passenger, an American, was startled by my appearance, as it looked like I had just woken up from a deep rest and was radiating energy.

One subject led to another, and before I could even understand why I was so radiant, he quipped to me that he was a sexual transmutation practitioner and made me realise that my three weeks of prayer and abstinence from all forms of desire, including sexual ones, had helped us bag the deal. Over the next few hours, I recapped the day's events to him, how we went all the way to the top of the 12 bidders from the bottom and won the prestigious contract.

I was aghast at the confidence I radiated and the psychological maturity I displayed during the negotiations with the young baron, which had allowed me to attain a higher realm of demeanour and be successful in bagging the contract. This immediately led me to a deeper understanding of another one of my father's positive affirmations.

Just to digress a bit at this point, I find myself going back in time to my childhood and recollecting the period when it went through an upheaval due to the tumultuous nature of my parents' relationship. Without taking sides, I must say that this tumult did affect our family. My parents went their own ways, and my father chose chastity for the rest of his life, which had a profound impact not only on my family but the many lives he touched.

He was a devout Catholic and fervent churchgoer who lived a simple life. He never longed for any materialistic pleasures and dedicated his entire time to work and family, besides the pursuit of spiritual solace. Over the next 30 years, my father continued to lead a life of praise and worship marked by his strong dedication to his profession and to the 100 families whose livelihoods depended on him.

As I grew and matured, I found it hard to believe that a person could strictly adhere to the principle of resisting all physical or materialistic desires. It was not just me but also my spouse who was curious about his ascetic life. In the face of the hordes of challenges within the industry that threatened to consume our organisation, how did he single-handedly and through force of will deal with all his professional, personal, and health issues? He survived the onslaught and came out victorious. Though life's trials had their own effects on his health and his age caught up with him, you could still see him glowing in a way that defied his age, which anyone would envy.

With his never-say-die attitude, even after a day's hectic work, a sleep-deprived night, or a visit to the mines, he would radiate energy to such an extent that people would continue to want to be by his side. He was extraordinary! It was hard for me to fathom how a man could radiate such energy, but my African sojourn led to my comprehension of another of my father's affirmations.

Dwelling deeper into the subject of sexual austerity, it is important to realise we live in an age of instant gratification. By not learning to delay gratification, in whatever form, we are creating a bad precedence for our minds and bodies. We are disconnected from our source of enlightenment and thereby succumb to the negative effects of pleasure and procrastination.

From a business management perspective, the concept of sexual austerity was new to me, and I scoffed at it initially. However, observing those who had resolved to follow the path of sexual austerity, I realised that it led to a form of eternal bliss, a state in which the full extent of one's creative energies if channelled could be used to achieve great success. People who practice sexual austerity work harder, mentally and physically, wake up early every morning and are more refined in areas of consciousness. If you can control your emotions, then you are powerful. Delaying gratification and transforming that energy into something productive and creative enables us to achieve success beyond the limits of our imagination. From static to motile, rudimentary to sophisticated, trivial to colossal, and mediocre to genius transformations were apparent for those who followed the path of sexual austerity.

In a world where sex has been so degraded, it's helpful to have a practice that encourages us to reassess our relationship with it, to understand desire and sexual energy. To lay it bare, the elderly co-passenger went on to elucidate that when one feels a strong sexual energy rise, one should just open oneself up and try to understand what the energy yearns for. It is often a craving for oneness or unity. By being still, allowing the energy to move as energy instead of being shaped by desire, consciously being with it in that way, we allow the energy to transform itself into a supernatural force. In simple words, one who masters his sexual energy is the master of his life.

My father was a preceptor and a living example of how one's sexual energy can be used to manifest your creative desires and set a roadmap for your destiny.

To summarise, it requires significant effort on our part to resist improper sexual urges and to refocus that energy elsewhere. If you develop the quality to refocus that energy, you will by no means ever fail.

Instinct Evens the Odds

Founders are often great storytellers because they're in the business of constantly selling a dream against all odds.

Jennifer Hyman

A couple of months into the new project with the East African client, I received a call from a friend in Thailand. I quickly surmised something was amiss from the feeble voice at the other end. The long-distance call was to brief me about our prospects for supplying equipment for a captive power plant intended for a major fabric brand in the Southeast Asian market.

The same friend had hosted me during one of my earlier trips to Thailand, and it went on to become a lasting friendship. Our conversation evoked memories about how time had flown ever since we last met in this mystical land. The vivid evocation of being enthralled by Thailand's hospitality, especially the ambience, Tuk-Tuks, exotic flora and fauna, temples with their glistening pinnacles, royal palaces adorned with intricate architecture while their gabled roofs and colossal spires that dominated the city skyline and last but foremost, gazing from afar the ubiquitous blobs of Buddhist monks clad in robes with hues of yellow, saffron and burgundy spread across the monasteries all of which had a tranquil yet pleasing effect on me.

My friend stated that the client was a bit sceptical of our capabilities, something that was not pleasant to my ears. The conversation veered around how one of my competitors had been trying to malign our painstakingly built reputation in the market by making false allegations against us without any merit or basis. With discussions lasting for over an hour, culminating in a satisfactory exchange of ideas, my organisation consented to send across an estimate for a dozen varieties of equipment that aimed at conveying the fuel for the power plant.

After a month and a half of pre-bid discussions, the preliminary rounds of negotiations commenced. It was during one of these meetings that I realised that something was terribly not working for us. The blatant lies by my competitor had spread without prejudice across the fabric brand.

I was left flabbergasted yet again when the client spoke about a communication they had received about us, indicating low-quality standards in our manufacturing. I found their claim and the fallacious inferences totally baseless and unjustifiable. I had neither expected one of my competitors to share this questionable piece of information nor imagined that a familiar face would be behind it all—a disgruntled official from the East African conglomerate. It's a small world indeed. I wondered how a person all the way across the world could be so devious and stoop so low to taint a reputed organisation. It also revealed my competitor's nefarious designs—the same competitor who had spread false rumours about my father being bedridden, leaving an ownership-driven organisation like ours rudderless. These maestros who were pulling the strings behind the scenes knew that my organisation had one of its best coxswains in me. Nevertheless, I briefed my family about the ploy and about how the competitor was vicious and unethical in his attempts to attack our organisation.

I recollect how my father would always enunciate the need to fight with will and courage—especially when the odds are stacked against you. After a taxing day at work, I got back home and ran my wife through the events that had transpired. We *instinctively* understood that it was of utmost prominence for me to be in Thailand to counter the false accusations the competitor had made by aligning with the disgruntled official from the African conglomerate. This was again a difficult time in my life, as my wife and I were expecting our second child, and we had just returned home after she had been hospitalised for a few days. My wife, without any further ado, encouraged me to take the very next flight to the mystical land that I cherished.

I immediately booked my tickets, hastily packed my bags, and left for the airport the same night. At the immigration counter, I was asked by the official about my date of return, and I handed over the boarding card for my return trip, which was less than 24 hours after my departure! The polite official asked me the place of visit, and I said Saraburi, Bangkok. He was quite puzzled about my travelling to another country for such a short duration and reminded me that I had just a few hours to accomplish what I intended to.

Nevertheless, I thought it was worth a shot since I had to return the same day for another important meeting the subsequent morning. After five hours of air travel, I was at the sprawling Suvarnabhumi Airport. Inside was a swarm of tourists, and there was chaos and commotion at the visa arrival counters. It took almost an hour for the visa application process, and then I was out to face the next big challenge awaiting me. Since time was precious, I hurriedly tried to get a cab, but to my dismay, the drivers were overcharging me and refused to travel by the meter. As I was unwilling to relent, a young woman police officer approached and enquired if anything was amiss. I briefed the officer about what was happening, following which she yelled at the cab drivers and managed to arrange for me a cab ride by meter.

After a two-and-a-half-hour drive, I arrived at the industrial town of Saraburi and checked into the hotel to freshen up; it was almost half-past eight. I then called up my client, who mentioned that he would send a chauffeur to pick me up from the hotel. After a quick shower, and heading out to the pickup junction, I began rehearsing in my mind what I would present to the client, oblivious to the actual importance of the next 30 minutes—my precious time in solitude. This was where another key element of my father's wisdom transpired.

As I was waiting for the chauffeur at the pickup point across the street, an aged Thai Buddhist monk walking by occupied the empty seat beside me. In his hands were prayer beads that he would use to meditate. The monk, who was en route to his monastery in the nearby hills, retired for the night at the same hotel.

We began a conversation while he was awaiting a bus to return to his remote town. Looking at his deep brown eyes and the regal smile on his face, I was certain he could sense a storm brewing in me. With a mere gaze and a smile, he could decipher a wide range of emotions in me, while offering a solution to the most complex of situations that I was encountering. He gently enquired about my visit to this land and shared a lot of his sacred wisdom.

He told me how Buddhist monks would traverse uncharted lands on the wings of hope. They would meditate and pray that their journeys would not be plagued by ill omens and, most importantly, that their philosophies of life would be understood, treasured, and leveraged by others for eternal happiness.

He further added that my instinct was razor-sharp in travelling all the way to Thailand and all that I needed was the will and courage to face the client.

A few minutes later, a young man came in enquiring about me, and I realised that he was the chauffeur. Before I bid adieu to the monk, he gently tapped my hand to reassure me and went on to say that the beauty of the moon could never be stolen. Awestruck, I realised that the monk was trying to convey that my true worth could never be blemished by my adversaries.

Just then I realised that another of my father's affirmations had come alive and that the previous 30 minutes had been truly insightful, with my gaining a lot of knowledge and wisdom from just a few minutes with the monk. I bid him goodbye, although with a heavy heart, as I knew that it was possible I would never see him again.

A quick drive took me to the fabric factory. I alighted from the car and shot straight for the security office. Since it was a visit on short notice and no appointment had been made, I handed my visiting card to the security personnel and said that I had come to meet the project manager. They asked me to fill in my credentials, explained a few procedures, and gave me protective gear to don. Suddenly, we heard a car approaching the entrance, alerting all the security personnel, who ran towards the gate. I realised their alacrity was not so much the result of a sense of urgency but sheer respect for the senior official entering the factory. While I went ahead and completed the entrance and safety procedures, someone called the security office and enquired about my presence.

I was a touch nervous and anxious since I had just a few hours to convince the client and catch my return flight. While I was being ushered into the conference room, I was contemplating about the monk and his wise words. The plant head and other officials were in the room, discussing something of prime importance. They greeted me as I took my seat on the opposite side of them. After a brief introduction, I started with the presentation about our company's expertise and proficiency, not realising that it would be the pitch of a lifetime, as I convinced the client of our capabilities.

Out of curiosity, I asked why they bought my competitor's claims about my firm's ostensibly poor track record in the East African project and went on to assure them that they had been tricked into believing we were incompetent. After the meeting concluded, I realised that the plant head was the same person who had been in the sedan that had driven past the security gates. He asked me to join him for a discussion after the meeting. In the minutes that followed, the fact that we were pioneers in this field finally struck him hard, and much to my surprise, he requested his team to visit my facility back home before visiting those of my competitors.

I quickly thanked the officials before I bid them adieu and began my long drive back to Bangkok to catch my return flight.

En route to the airport, I pondered about another of my father's affirmations, which had instilled the zeal to succeed against all odds in me. The old monk, I believe, was *sent* to give me the courage and fortitude to overcome this precarious situation.

A couple of weeks later, officials from the fabric brand visited my production facility and was amazed by our quality, competence, and expertise. I successfully inked the contract and was overwhelmed by the fact that I had outwitted my competitors, teaching them the lesson of a lifetime, one that ensured they would never imagine doing the same thing again. The officials, though quite apologetic, also added that they were impressed with me for having travelled all the way just to convey the message that one should never trust someone blindly—it was the greatest lesson of their lives.

Contrary to my competitor's expectations, we proved them wrong and bagged the deal. We also exposed the competitor's deviousness in joining forces with the East African official to try and tarnish my firm's brand.

The crowning achievement was not just the clinching of the contract but also the silencing of my naïve competitor and the disgruntled official of the African conglomerate. Well! The journey to Thailand would not have eventuated, nor would I have triumphed, if it wasn't for another of my father's affirmations and the monk's wise words of wisdom.

***

Wine, Women, Wealth & Wisdom

I make myself rich by making my wants few.

Henry David Thoreau

The title startled you, didn't it? I have a fine reason for bringing this topic up.

A couple of months into the successful execution of the project in Thailand, I was invited yet again to bid for another upcoming project with the African conglomerate.

Having survived the imperils of the nefarious competitor and the disgruntled officials of the conglomerate who were cognizant of being exposed for trying to tarnish my organisation's repute with the Thai fabric brand, I, being deeply incited, decided to take them head-on.

A short drive from my hotel, deep in the woods, not far from the central business district, was located a beautiful, gated property of the young baron's family, nicknamed the Seven Hills, as it housed seven different mansions. These vintage manors, suffused with history and folklore reminiscent of their original European owners who resided at this enormous property lingered on, long after their departure from the East African nation. It was during their heydays that the Caucasians began building their heavenly abode. Well, during the mid-nineteenth century, not long before they could cherish the fruits of their labour, the seven families had to relocate to their country of origin in fear of civil strife by the neighbouring country's dictator whose atrocities and blatant wielding of power, especially against foreigners, cast a spell on those who travelled far and wide in search of a future in this pristine part of the world. The baron's family had then bought the property from the erstwhile owners who had curated this beautiful piece of marvel, inspiring many to be enthralled with nature.

Driving through the entrance to the location of the meeting, as briefed to me by one of the security guards at the entrance gate, I noticed the serene surroundings and quickly alighted from my car to get a glimpse of this magnificent yet peaceful property.

On strolling amidst the tall and well-grown trees, I witnessed the property swarmed with different species of caterpillars and leaf insects to colourful butterflies. It was not just the colourful wing-flapping creatures, but soon I was captivated by the richness and splendour of the floral beauty. The property was teeming with life both above and under the ground. I was deeply reverent of the founder and his family, especially for their love of nature preservation. A few minutes' walk got me to the fringes of the wooded reserve and into the vast sprawling ornamental grass lawns, well-pruned shrubs, and hedges, on the opposite end of which stood the beautiful seven independent mansions. The pristine beauty and the tranquil atmosphere were an absolute treat to the eyes.

On entering the beautiful yet secluded bungalow that I was directed to, I noticed that the mansion had been converted into a personal office space for the young baron.

Walking through the opulent office, I saw the head of the disgruntled coterie seated at the entrance of the boardroom. On greeting the official, he smiled back faintly, knowing how hard it was to rile up someone as invincible as me. Seated not far from our discussions was the nefarious competitor who seemed all the more riled up.

After a brief chat outside the boardroom and a few hours wait, I was called in for the meeting presided over by the young baron himself. Notwithstanding that the boardroom was filled with many annoyed officials with numerous bouts of unwarranted complaints, which I was reluctant to counter, I remained calm and played my game smartly.

After spending an entire evening filled with discussions and some arduous negotiations, I went on to bag my first multi-million-dollar deal with the group. It was almost half-past ten at night and the group's owner quickly congratulated me on securing the order with a warm handshake, which ended in a hug, ensuring the deal was finalised. I was humbled by the gesture of the young, third-generation entrepreneur, who stood up to hand over the formal order for the project.

However, in hindsight, I realised that this was the beginning of another phase of the myriad of challenges that I would have to face with his subordinates at the factory. Well, that's a story for another chapter.

After the signing formalities and protocols were completed, we exited the bungalow and I was yet again humbled when the owner, who, while entering his posh SUV, asked if I needed a ride to my hotel. I was in awe of his hospitality, which I later understood was passed down to him by his grandparents. I politely declined the offer, as I wanted to avoid another brush with the already envious officials.

A few moments later, my cab arrived, and it was almost 11 p.m. The drive through the thick dark woods got me to the CBD, which appeared like a train steaming out of a dark tunnel, with a sudden burst of bright lights striking my eyes. Just as I reached the hotel, another vendor who had bagged a contract from the same group greeted and congratulated me, which I reciprocated. He checked if we could head out for a celebration, to which my chauffeur responded by suggesting that we hit the neighbouring casino, as it was safer, with the food and drinks on the house! We took his advice and left for the casino. A minute's drive got us to one of the most opulent dens around.

It was one of the largest casinos in the East African city. We paid the entrance fee, took a few chips and headed indoors, which was atmospheric with loud music. The smell and smoke of African cigars lingered in the air, with hordes of gamblers being entertained by the hosts.

It was a packed house and the tropical décor around the gambling den mesmerised me. It was garish and over the top, which was why it drew scores of gamblers. Many hit the dance floor and it was an absolute blast. People visit casinos to unwind and test their luck against the hands of fate, and on that particular night, I too was no exception.

We quickly sat at one of the tables that had two vacant seats, unaware that it was a high-stakes table.

Nevertheless, it never occurred to us to change our minds, since we had both clinched high-value contracts, and it was a special night.

While I was familiar with five-card poker, I needed a helping hand with the three-card poker game which was a bit confusing and difficult for me to comprehend as I wasn't familiar with its set of rules. As I was getting accustomed to the game, a young woman of Indian origin saw me struggling and offered to help. It was not long before I started winning, with her as my lucky mascot. And after I had won a few thousand dollars, it was time for the dealer to change.

A waiter quickly got me a platter of fritters and a glass of Sauvignon blanc. While sipping my drink, I noticed a gambler near me, who resembled a warlord, with at least $20,000 worth of chips on the table. He appeared drunk, arrogant and boisterous, drinking and eating merrily while boasting about his previous win—a royal flush.

The air was electric, as most of the gamblers seemed to be winning, and the night was young and vibrant. Just then, the new dealer, an extremely attractive woman, came by and started the card count. As she shuffled the cards with ease, I figured out that she was a seasoned dealer. The gusty gambler was constantly chatting with her, and I realised that they were familiar with each other.

Focusing was a challenge for all the players at the table, since Mr. Gusty never ceased chatting for even a second. A quick glance at the dealer made it clear how terrified and uncomfortable she was. I looked at my good Samaritan friend, who winked at me, indicating that I was to ignore the unruly gambler's behaviour.

The game resumed and we started winning again. Our spirits were high. Mr. Gutsy once again struck a full house and won a few thousand dollars. He threw the highest-value chip to the dealer as a proposition to which she handed it back to him with a grin on her face.

I quickly turned to the Indian woman and asked what had happened. She said, *'Money can't buy everything.'* I later realised the $100 chip was an indirect effort to solicit the dealer to spend the night with the gambler.

A sudden thought crossed my mind about the gambler's wayward behaviour with regards to money, wine and women. While he had all the wealth in the world, he did not know how to play his cards right, be true to one woman, or hold a glass of wine.

I recollected what my father told me about young boys of my time. As teenagers, we bunk classes to party and drink wine. On the way to puberty, our priorities change to women. By our mid-30s, we seek wealth. By the time we gain wisdom, we have outlived ourselves.

My father was never against preferences for wine, women, wealth or wisdom—it was the sequence that he expected me to emulate, for my father believed that, if a man had gained enough wisdom, he would know how to use his wealth or the wealth he inherited; he would know to respect a woman and be true to one woman; and, finally, he would evolve into a connoisseur of wine.

Before I called it a night, another of my father's affirmations, about how a man should prioritise these four essentials, came to mind. It was in the following order—wisdom, wealth, women and wine. This affirmation brings to mind the image of the prodigal son who has everything going for him but loses it all as he lacks wisdom and squanders his wealth on wine and women. And when wisdom strikes, he returns to his father's love.

If you had to choose between wealth and wisdom, which one would you choose and why? While the question may be subjective, it highlights a key facet of life. Wealth is something that gradually meets your needs; if you are greedy, no amount will suffice. Wealth, while desirable, is fleeting and ephemeral. It is much more extrinsic, whereas wisdom is intrinsic and timeless.

Becoming wise might take months, if not years, but you'll eventually get there if you keep at it. If you are endowed with immense knowledge, you will be asked to lead and pave the path towards the betterment of people around you. When you are wise, your understanding of any given situation adds a certain depth to your insights. Wealth, beauty, and materialistic things, though not essential, are byproducts of wisdom. Beauty fades and so does materialism, simply because it cannot brave the ravages of time, unlike wisdom.

This brings me to the last and one of my Father's most vital of affirmations - *taking everyone along* - which is crucial to becoming a truly successful entrepreneur. Something he accomplished extremely well during his four-decade-long journey at the helm of the modest yet great institution that he founded.

Taking Everyone Along

The greatest ability in business is to get along with others and to influence their actions.

John Hancock

On the last leg of my African sojourn, discussions with the young baron concluded a couple of days prior to its scheduled wrap-up meet. I had two full days and two full nights to kill before I returned home. Unable to reschedule my flight tickets due to the peak festive and holiday season rush, besides the airlines charging an exorbitant rescheduling fee. I decided to stay back and unwind, though my family was coaxing me to return home, probably sensing that I was weary of my hectic business tours.

Lonely and bored, I decided to head out to explore the natural scenic beauty of the countryside. On enquiring at the travel desk about the various tourist attractions the city was famous for, I was astonished on being informed that the capital city had a wildlife sanctuary in its backyard. I quickly chanced upon this rare, once-in-a-lifetime opportunity, and not wanting to let it go in vain. I began to explore every single tour operator that gave me the most exhilarating tour package while visiting the sanctuary.

Without further ado, having finalised my guide and tour operator, I made a beeline for an overnight stay at one of East Africa's most treasured wildlife sanctuaries that was at the edge of the bustling city capital. Nicknamed the Kifaru Ark which, during the last few decades, it translated to a haven for the great black rhino, something wildlife enthusiasts and nature conservationists could cherish as a result of their assiduous dedication and hard work.

Having visited many such sanctuaries around the world, this visit was unlike any of my past visits, as it culminated in a sense of gratitude, feeling empowered and enriched by the experience of sharing insights with remote cultures and tribes further witnessing the diversity of wildlife in all its resplendence and glory.

A three-hour-long drive from the central business district got me to my inn where I was to spend the night amongst nature and wildlife. The place was perched above the rugged hills overlooking the great Nakuru Lake that was at the fringes of this great sanctuary. The inn was set amidst a blend of rustic luxury, infinite views of flora and fauna, and nourishing native folklore all of which was entwined with nature.

After settling down in my plush room and a scrumptious lunch overlooking the boundless flora and fauna, I headed to the game reserve for an early evening safari with my tour guide and driver, along with a couple of other tourists who, too, appeared stunned and astonished upon witnessing the splendorous diversity of this wildlife in all its grandeur.

As we delved from the fringes, deep into the breathtaking game reserve, we got to a breezy, picturesque spot. The guide quickly instructed the driver to turn off the engine of our hard-top. A moment later, there was an abrupt silence from the loud engine rattle. This was when we realised that the air was soaked with the sounds of almost every living creature in this sanctuary except for humans. From harmonious resonances of birds chirping and calling, hyenas laughing, and insects trilling, to the echoes of winds whistling through the grass plains and savannahs, it appeared as though the forests, too, were pulsating from the sounds that permeated this lush green promised land.

I was awestruck by the sheer spectacle of nature that God had created. The generous abundance of flora and fauna was for everyone to see and feel—untouched for over a billion years, ever since our planet came into existence.

Encountering the majestic rhino, buffaloes, wildebeest, elusive leopards, lakes painted in pink from the migratory flamingo, and a wide array of other fascinating species, we retired for the night at our plush yet rustic manor. As I sank onto my feather bed, enthralled by what I had witnessed, amidst the silence all around me, the night was still; it was as though every living creature had paused in the darkness.

Early the next morning, I was awakened by the deafening sound of my telephone ringing; it was a wake-up call from my hotel reception to witness wildlife once again in all its fury.

After an hour-long drive into the deep, while witnessing the growing hues of orange over the horizon, we noticed the silhouette of a giant creature that appeared to get bigger with its every move. The driver of our hard-top quickly shut the engine off, citing danger. Just then, the creature approaching us paused with a shudder. It was obviously enraged by the sound of the rattling engine; I guess our guide and driver knew very well of the giant creature's dislike of the sounds of rattle. The beast, swaying sidewards, displayed its majestic horns in the shadow, revealing its identity. It was the endangered black rhino, a prominent attraction of the game reserve and the largest of the big four that the wildlife reserve was famous for.

We hovered around for a few more minutes, getting a better glimpse of the majestic creature as the layers of orange from the sunrise grew brighter further illuminating everything in its path. It was the most breathtaking view that I had witnessed.

The guide froze on witnessing this majestic yet humble creature. He sat still with an array of emotions that were obviously visible to all. It appeared as though his eyes were about to burst into a valley of tears. I sensed something amiss and gently patted his shoulders. I was spot on. Just as he looked at me, there were tears rolling down his cheeks. I ignored his emotions and gave it time to settle down for a while. It was soul-tumbling for all of us to see our tour guide in a state of seemingly endless grief.

On inquiring about our guide's emotional outburst during the early morning sunrise, he narrated how he witnessed the last male white rhino in the neighbouring sanctuary being "put down" to end its suffering. It was also an end to an evolutionary thread that spanned billions of years. He further elucidated how he and many of the game rangers could do nothing but bear witness to this horrendous outcome that was predominantly due to poaching which was still rife in these sanctuaries and the conservationists could do nothing much to preserve what was left of the flora and fauna.

The great white rhino was now extinct, and it was painful to see, how we humans were responsible for the extinction of one of God's creations and it is only a matter of time before many creatures we witnessed would go through the same fate.

While speaking his heart out, a grin on the guide's face displayed a ray of hope. Suddenly, there appeared to be a commotion amongst the avians nearby. Pointing out to the rhino at the fringes of the lake, he described how Mother Earth had an answer to almost all of nature's greatest conundrums. He spoke greatly for the tiny blobs of brown and red that were perched all over the rhino. It was the Oxpecker, also called "the rhino's guard", which formed a symbiotic relationship with the majestic creatures. These wingmen, besides pecking on the parasites and ticks that agitate the rhino, also help in swiftly sounding an alarm to the poor-sighted rhino as and when they sense danger closing in. In fact, the commotion we witnessed was all about a pack of hyenas approaching the rhino's calf. The guide further briefed how these winged creatures even signalled poachers approaching from afar. I was mesmerised by the sheer cohabitation of how different species could live in such harmony amongst themselves and nature, whereas we humans, as one species lived with so much hatred and contempt.

The ice-cold morning wind caressing my hair while riding through, in the open-top land cruiser, I realised we were near the fringes of one of God's greatest manifestations. It was all the more humbling to realise that we were just a speck of dust in this universe, and yet we live lives in antagonism.

As we cruised through the forest, every tourist participating in the open-top safari was humbled by the sights and sounds all around. It was at a particular spot when the guide slowed down on hearings the chirps and barks and my heart skipped a beat as we sensed it being a sign that danger was nearing. It was the majestic lion in all its magnificence. It was such a joyful sight to behold, witnessing nature in its bare form and with tears, I reflected on how much we had contributed towards the destruction of this beautiful yet lonely living planet. Without a doubt, we are the worst kind of species to have walked the Earth. As a notable individual had said, *'Every animal in the animal kingdom should be allowed to procreate and hunt and complete the circle of life.'*

In my opinion, nature has taken cognisance as to why humans are still in existence. If there is to be one takeaway from this book, I ask every reader to visit at least one of the few breathtaking natural wonders—the Masai Mara in Africa, the Rann of Kutch in India, the Norwegian Northern Lights Wolf Sanctuary, the Great Barrier Reef, the Grand Canyon, and the like. Only then can we fathom what creation is all about and comprehend the greatness of nature and how we have been unfair towards it. It will become clear that our lack of fairness towards our fellow human beings is firmly rooted in our actions against nature itself.

When we reached a particular spot that was deeper inside than the fringes of the reserve, our Masai guide pointed to the matriarch of a herd of about 30 elephants and explained how she stood her ground, risking everything for the sake of the herd.

This reminded me of another of my father's affirmations, on the responsibility of taking everyone along, just like the elephant families with their matriarchal heads. An older, experienced female elephant leads the herd in plotting their journey across the forest, negotiating large rivers and guiding them to green pastures. I could relate this to my father's affirmations or the story of any great business house of the world—the main character is responsible for taking everyone along, and no business house has ever survived without direction. And the guide in the remotest African game reserve knew it best. He further briefed us on how a nearby Masai tribal leader and his wives stayed together with their children and the entire clan—making do with what they had, no matter how little, and living through life's greatest challenges with their joy intact, something unimaginable in the 'developed' world.

Before I could end my journey, the elderly Masai guide took us to a nearby village and introduced us to the African tribe. With goats bleating, men protecting the livestock, women milking cows, children hunting tiny insects; we were all amazed to see how they lived in harmony; though they were materially less fortunate than many, their lives were filled with contentment, unlike many of us who have everything we desire but are devoid of empathy, compassion, and love for our fellow beings.

We then reached the drop-off point, and the Masai wished us Ubuntu. The word sounded familiar. Upon our inquiring about it, he narrated different versions of its story. I give my version below, which I recently stumbled upon.

> *An anthropologist proposed a game to a group of African tribal children.*
>
> *He placed a basket of sweets near a tree, made the children stand 100 metres away and announced that whoever reached the basket first would get all the sweets in the basket.*
>
> *He then said, 'Ready, steady, go!'*
>
> *Do you know what the children did? They held each other's hands, ran together towards the tree, divided the sweets equally among themselves, ate them and enjoyed themselves.*
>
> *The anthropologist asked them why they did so.*
>
> *They answered, 'Ubuntu,' which meant, 'How can one be happy when others are sad?'*
>
> *Ubuntu in their language means, 'I am because we are.'*
>
> *A strong message for all generations.*

As humans, let us nurture this attitude and spread happiness wherever we go.

Let's have an 'Ubuntu' life.

I AM BECAUSE WE ARE. SO LET'S TAKE EVERYONE ALONG.

This was my last trip to the African land. I never had the opportunity to go back, although I eagerly wish to even today. Neither did I get to say goodbye to the young baron. I miss my hour-long conversations with him.

Nevertheless, I hope my father's ten affirmations, which made themselves felt in such a transcendental way during my great African journey, will play an impactful role not just in your life but in the life of every person you meet in your journey.

Until we meet again on my next journey...Ubuntu!

***

Closing

I realised that taking ownership of the project resulted in a dramatic increase in the efficiency of my workforce, thereby bringing about great closures for clients.

How did I do that? I learnt that by investing in people, clients, and society, I could help the company leverage greater insights and establish a strong work culture, while being held together by a firm ethos.

I found it was indeed a great honour for me to be constantly striving to identify and convert opportunities for us to shape the future and help our clients create value for their stakeholders. People, technology, and innovation are some of the aspects that I focused on in the years that followed, with a view to ensuring the responsible and sustainable growth of the firm, our clients, as well as our society.

I managed to take the time to consolidate our learnings and plan for the future, setting out a clear roadmap for how we would take the organisation to the next level. We reinforced our team by adding people with core competencies that naturally brought in the required domain knowledge and expertise to the organisation. Next, we built great industry relationships, to be a trusted point of contact for businesses.

Personally, it's been a transformational journey for me. I have seen my company emerge as a leader, admired and respected within the industry and by all stakeholders. I owe my deepest gratitude to my father and also to the board, management, and staff of my company for their support during my trials and tribulations.

In the process of writing this book, I've learnt many lessons, but most importantly, I've learnt to see the wisdom behind my father's words of affirmation!

This book is a tribute to the Great African Land and the indomitable spirit of its People.

My journey continues Belabouring the Obvious…

***

www.ingramcontent.com/pod-product-compliance
Lightning Source LLC
LaVergne TN
LVHW091327150826
845673LV00006B/1795

* 9 7 9 8 8 8 8 1 5 3 0 2 4 *